"WITH THEIR USUAL ARDOR"

Scituate, Rhode Island

and the

American Revolution

Robert Grandchamp

HERITAGE BOOKS
2025

HERITAGE BOOKS

AN IMPRINT OF HERITAGE BOOKS, INC.

Books, CDs, and more—Worldwide

For our listing of thousands of titles see our website
at
www.HeritageBooks.com

Published 2025 by
HERITAGE BOOKS, INC.
Publishing Division
5810 Ruatan Street
Berwyn Heights, MD 20740

Heritage Books by the author:
From Providence to Fort Hell: Letters from Company K, Seventh Rhode Island Volunteers
"In Te Domine Speramus": Essays on Rhode Island Military History
*"Like Sheep at the Slaughter": A Statistical
History of the Fourth Rhode Island Volunteers*
*"Now Show Them What Rhode Island Can Do!": An Annotated
Bibliography of Rhode Island Civil War Sources*
"We Lost Many Brave Men": A Statistical History of the Seventh Rhode Island Volunteers
"With their usual ardor": Scituate, Rhode Island and the American Revolution

Cover illustration, entitled "Farmer's Call: April 20, 1775,"
by Joyce Knight Townsend

International Standard Book Number
Paperbound: 978-0-7884-4091-5

To my mother and grandmother, who kept the history alive.
And to the memory of the fifty-two officers and men of
Captain Joseph Knight's Second Company of Minutemen,
who answered the call on April 19, 1775.
Let this volume be their memorial.

"I have no doubt that your officers and men will exert themselves upon this occasion with their usual ardor."

–Governor Nicholas Cooke
December 19, 1775

CONTENTS

ILLUSTRATIONS

ACKNOWLEDGMENTS

This work is the result of three years of arduous research into one town's contributions to the American Revolution. I am especially grateful to the following for their assistance:

Shirley Arnold, for providing me unlimited access to her treasure of Knight material. Mrs. Arnold is a treasure of Scituate. To her a deep debt is owed.

Scott Donahue, of Tew's Company, Second Rhode Island Regiment for providing information on his ancestor, Palmer Tanner of Scituate.

Andrew Fredricks, of Tew's Company, Second Rhode Island Regiment, for sharing his knowledge on the Rhode Island Continentals.

Caleb Horton, my pard. He brought Sergeant Benjamin Boss back to life.

Brian Mellow, of Tew's Company, Second Rhode Island Regiment for providing invaluable material pertaining to the Battle of Prudence Island.

Roy Najecki, of the 40th Regiment of Foot, for providing an excellent overview of the Battle of Rhode Island, and the British forces in Newport.

Peg Pinkey, Town Records Clerk in Scituate, for putting up with my constant visits and "rummaging" around the Scituate Town Records.

INTRODUCTION

I n April 1775, a small group of men from Scituate, Rhode Island, left their farms and homes and responded to their country's call. Men from Scituate would again serve with distinction; in December 1775 they would save Providence from capture, and in 1776 they would help drive the British out of Narragansett Bay. In 1778 they would face their greatest challenge, as they marched to face the enemy in their own state. The Scituate Militia was one that could always be depended upon.

Scituate also contributed over one hundred men to the Continental Army through the Second Rhode Island Regiment. These men would fight with George Washington in such actions as New York, Red Bank, Valley Forge, Monmouth, Rhode Island, Springfield, and Yorktown.

In the village of Hope was a large iron works, called the Hope Furnace. This company would cast over one thousand cannon and tens of thousands of cannonballs for the Revolutionary effort. These cannon would prove decisive on many a battlefield.

The men and women who stayed behind also contributed greatly to the war effort. The men participated in such diverse efforts as making firearms and salt, to collecting taxes for soldiers' wages, while the women of Scituate made necessary items for the soldiers, and maintained the many farms and shops while their husbands were at war.

For Scituate, the American Revolution was an event that the whole town would support as its men, and women fought for their independence from Great Britain. After nearly ten years, that independence would finally be gained, but at a terrible cost.

In this volume the author has attempted, to bring full justice to the deeds of the citizens of Scituate, and their contributions to the Revolution. It is the authors hope that this work will serve as a fitting tribute to their service, and sacrifice.

Robert Grandchamp
Warwick, Rhode Island
August 29, 2005

In Te Domine Speramus

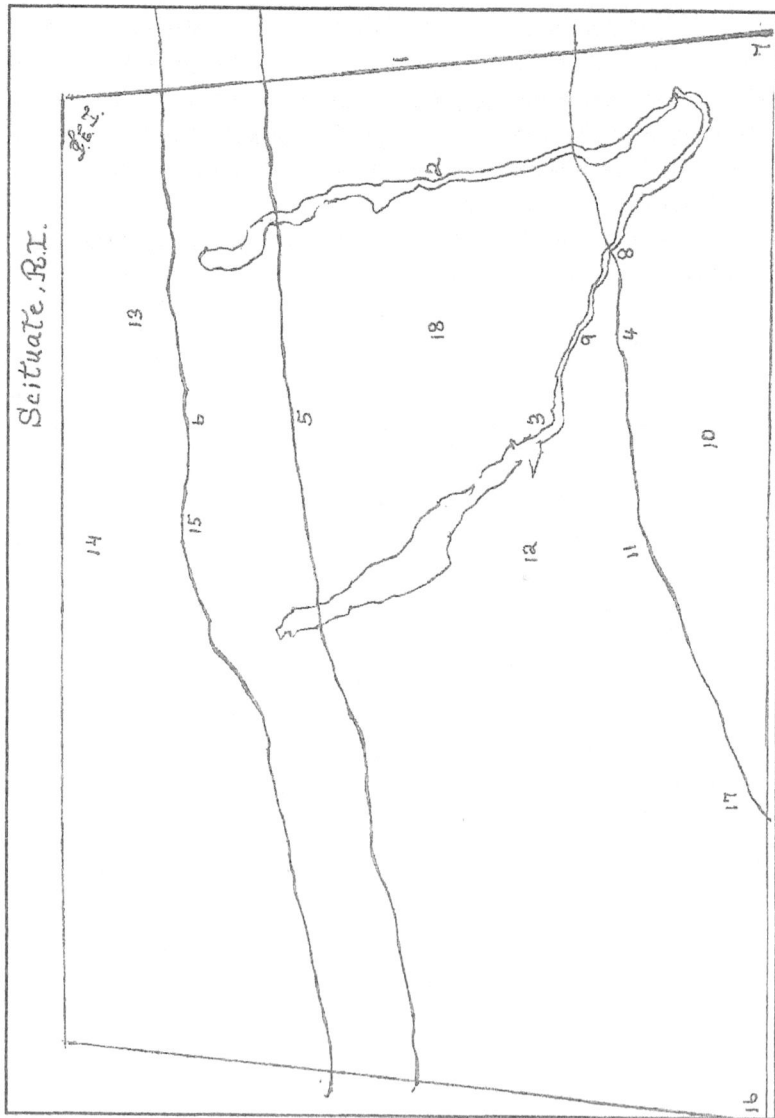

Map by
Joyce Knight Townsend

Key:
1. Seven Mile Line
2. Pawtuxet River
3. Ponagansett River
4. Plainfield Pike
5. Central Pike
6. Danielson Pike
7. Hope Village and
   Hope Furnace
8. Richmond
9. Angell Tavern
10. South Scituate
11. Knight Farm
12. Rockland
13. North Scituate
14. Scituate Beacon on
    Chopmist Hill
15. Great House
16. Moosup Valley
17. Vernon
18. Wilbur Hollow

CHAPTER ONE

Scituate, Rhode Island

S atuit is an Algonquin word meaning cold brook. So describes a town located seven miles west of Providence, Rhode Island. This town is bounded by a large forest intermittent with meadows and ponds, encompassed by the Pawtuxet and Ponagansett Rivers. The landscape had been carved out by glaciers during the last Ice Age, leaving behind large masses of granite and iron in its soil. Three main roads ran through this town, the Central, Danielson, and Plainfield Pikes. Most of its inhabitants were apple or dairy farmers, with some tradesmen, mechanics, and gentlemen. The majority of the inhabitants were of Puritan stock, some of their ancestors having come to America in 1620 aboard the *Mayflower*. By 1775 the roots of this town's inhabitants were already buried deep in the rocky soil of western Rhode Island; they would be hard to remove. This town is Scituate, Rhode Island.

Scituate was first settled in 1651 by John Matthewson, who built a small mud hut in the northeastern corner of the town, along the shores of Moswansicut Pond. Matthewson became a trapper, and traded with the natives. The closest civilization was Boston, to which he could walk in two days.[1] Prior to this, the only inhabitants of the area had been a small band of native people known as the Tunkies, who numbered around four hundred and lived along the Ponagansett River. During King Philip's War, Metacom and the Nipmuc sachems, met at a place known as the Indian Bowl near Tunk Hill. No action of any kind, though, took place here during that conflict.[2] In 1708 several families moved to the area from Scituate, Massachusetts, bringing with them the town name. In 1730 a line seven miles west of Providence was set out, dividing the two towns.[3] By 1774 the town population was 3,601 and of these, 806 were of military age and able to bear arms.

Amongst the town population were thirty African slaves, and no Native Americans.[4]

Amongst the families moving to Scituate was the Knights. They traced a long line of descent in England, and arrived in the New World in 1632 when Richard Knight escaped England to avoid persecution. He would eventually establish himself as a minister in Newbury, Massachusetts, and would marry Sarah Rogers, of *Mayflower* stock. In 1705 their descendents moved to Scituate and settled on Tunk Hill, where they planted a large apple orchard and operated a sawmill.[5]

By 1770 Scituate was a large town divided into many villages with names such as Ashland, Hope, Kent, Richmond, Rockland, and Wilbur Hollow. Each village was a unique place, and had its own industry and flavor. The central part of each village was the tavern; here local business was transacted, and social events were held. The Angell Tavern, located in the village of Richmond along the Plainfield Pike, was one of these places. Thomas Angell built this tavern in 1710. It served as an armory, meeting hall, and post office. In addition it was a very popular eating and drinking establishment servicing those on their way to Connecticut. C.C. Beaman, in his *Historical Address*, leaves a very detailed description of the tavern:

> It was two stories high, with the eaves of the front extending a few feet, forming a little shelter in stormy weather. On the western end was a very huge stone-chimney, forming a wall for that end of the building. There was also back of the main building, an addition sloping down from the main roof to form a kitchen, closet and bed-room, one story high, which being old and out of repair, was taken down in 1823. The house had three narrow windows, with small panes of glass on the lower front, and four of the same description above, with one at the east end. The front door was at the western extremity of the part facing on the road. As you entered, a door on the right hand of the passage opened upon the bar-room, a large square room, and leading out of it, the entire length of the remaining fore part of the house was a sitting-room, used in later years, if not before, for a bed-room. Back of the barroom was a kitchen, a large square room, which had been as large again

The farm of John Potter in South Scituate. The farm was typical of most Scituate dairy farms. Author's Collection.

before the addition was removed. A bedroom was at one end of it, nearly corresponding in size to the sitting room, directly behind which it stood. The only pair of stairs to the upper rooms, ascended from the kitchen at the west end. Three bedrooms were on the east end, and all the rest of the second floor, with the exception of a sleeping chamber over the front entry, was a hall for dancing and public meetings.

Being situated on the Plainfield Pike, the Angell Tavern served all of Scituate. The militia met and held their drills on a large field near the tavern. The most important function of the Angell Tavern however, was as a venue for town meetings. Here the cherished ideals of freedom were maintained, and the principles of New England democracy prevailed: that all men were equal, and that liberty was a God-given right. Many important events would transpire here during the Revolution.[6]

During the long years of war that lay ahead, the people of Scituate would never falter to do their duty. Amongst those people were groups of men known as the training bands or the militia. They would have a key role in events to come.

CHAPTER TWO

The Militia

D uring the 1700s, there was no standing army to protect the people of Scituate. For the purpose of protecting the town, Scituate relied upon its own citizens in organized forces called training bands or militia. These forces were composed of all able-bodied males aged sixteen to fifty. They were first organized by the earliest settlers for protection from Indians, and later the French.

The Scituate Militia first saw service during the French and Indian War, in the 1758 Crown Point Campaign. Scituate provided a company to the Rhode Island Battalion fighting on the frontier near the Hudson River. Many of these men would be given land grants for their services, and would settle in southern Vermont.[1]

In the late 1750s, Scituate reorganized the town militia into four companies, by dividing the town into four sections. The First Company, comprised men from the villages of Kent, Rockland, Richmond, and South Scituate. The Second Company was recruited from southwestern Scituate, while the Fourth Company was recruited in northwestern Scituate. The Third Company was recruited in the village of North Scituate.

A member of the First Company was a farmer named Joseph Knight. Knight was born on May 1, 1740 in Cranston, Rhode Island; he was already a fifth generation New Englander. At an early age his family removed to the Tunk Hill area of Scituate, and built a large house. In 1763 his father gave him the family apple farm, which most of the family worked upon, and he gave his brother Jonathan control of the large sawmill upon the property. The Knights' main income source was from purchasing land and clearing the trees, then selling the land to new owners and selling the trees as lumber.

In 1765, Joseph married his first cousin, Elizabeth Knight; together they had six children. In 1766 he became interested in military affairs, and was commissioned an ensign in the First Company of Militia. He was promoted to lieutenant in 1769, and to captain in 1774. Captain Knight and his men would be heard from many times during the Revolution.[2]

In 1774 the Scituate Militia supplied four companies to the Providence County Regiment. With growing tensions between the Colonies and the Crown, the Town of Scituate decided to reorganize its militia. On December 5, 1774, a town meeting was held at the Angell Tavern and the militia was reorganized. The First Company was divided to form the Fifth Company. Both companies, however, recruited from the same area, and men often transferred between the two. The Second Company was divided to form the Sixth Company, which recruited from the Chopmist Hill area. The Third Company of Cranston, located in the western part of that town became the Seventh Company, and comprised men from the village of Hope, as well as present day Fiskeville.[3]

Also created at the meeting was an Independent Company called the Scituate Hunters. This company was chartered by the Rhode Island General Assembly, and would be limited to four officers and eighty men, under Captain Joseph Kimball. Their charter opened with these words:

> Whereas the Preservation of this Colony in time War depends under God, and under the Military skill, and Discipline of its inhabitants.

The company was required to meet four times a year for training, and its members were heavily fined for missing a field day. The Scituate Hunters were considered an Independent Company, but would be under the command of the field officers "of the Third Battalion in the County of Providence." The company was also assigned a position on the right flank of the battalion, which was considered a great honor.[4]

With the additional four companies in Scituate, the town petitioned the Colony for permission to create its own battalion within the Providence County Brigade. The petition was granted, and the Scituate companies became the Third Providence County Regiment. Together with the First Regiment from Providence,

Johnston, and Cranston, and the Second Regiment from Cumberland, Gloucester, and Smithfield. The three regiments formed the Providence County Brigade, under Brigadier General Christopher Lippitt.[5]

The militia was organized in the common New England democratic style, everyone, regardless of rank or status had a voice in the decisions of the company or regiment. With the forming of the Third Providence County Regiment, Scituate held an election for the field officers. William West was elected Colonel, Ezekiel Cornell as Lieutenant Colonel, and John Colwell was elected Major. All were members of the Town Council and were prominent politicians in the town. Militarily, all had seen service during the French and Indian War, fighting on the New York frontier.[6]

In January 1775, the Rhode Island General Assembly voted to enlist a quarter of the state militia to become minutemen. These men would meet a half day every two weeks for drill, and would be paid two shillings for each day of service. The requirement to enlist the minutemen consisted of enlisting the young able bodied men in each company, who needed to be ready to muster within fifteen minutes of being notified. In Scituate two companies were selected to become minutemen. These were the Third Company of Militia which became the First Company of Minutemen, while Captain Knight's First Company of Militia became the Second Company of Minutemen. These men would truly live up to their name in the months ahead.[7]

With their militia reorganized, the men of Scituate spent the winter drilling, and organizing their equipment, for they knew that years of growing tension would soon escalate into war. And their skill with firearms and military discipline would prove decisive in the coming storm.

CHAPTER THREE

Arms, Equipment, and Organization

T he men of the Scituate Militia were citizen soldiers, and their weapons, and training were unique to their New England surroundings. The majority of the men in Scituate were apple and dairy farmers, and their dress and equipment often reflected their social standing.

Training in the Scituate Militia was often as much of a holiday as it was to learn military discipline. Each company drilled together once a month, while the battalion drilled four times per year.[1] During training day the taverns would open their doors, and the rum and flip would flow freely as the men attempted to learn the military movements of the period. The last Monday in April was set aside as election day, when the men would vote in the new officers. Though most officers were voted to their rank, they could also be promoted by political appointment or for gallantry in action. By tradition, the new officers had to purchase drinks for all those who voted for them. Each company was allotted one captain, lieutenant, ensign, and drummer, as well as two sergeants and corporals; many, however, exceeded the allotment.[2]

The officers and men drilled using *The Manual Exercise as Ordered by His Majesty in 1764;* the standard British army drill manual of the time. The *1764 Manual* was designed for fighting on open fields, and would prove totally ineffective for the type of warfare fought in North America. Many militia officers further modified the drill by forming open order. At open order the company would spread out at several paces distance between each man, and the men would fight in teams of two with their file partner, so one of them always had his musket loaded. Open order allowed a company to fight effectively in the forest, while still maintaining a military formation.[3] Relief to the officers using the *1764 Manual* came in 1775 when Colonel Timothy Pickering of the Massachusetts Militia published *An Easy Plan for the Discipline of a Militia*. Pickering presented a much-simplified version of the *1764 Manual*, as well as the duties of an officer. This book would prove invaluable to many officers in creating an effective company.[4]

The typical dress of a member of the Scituate Militia included a broad-brimmed or a cocked military-looking hat. Scituate farms produced large amounts of linen, which was used to make shirts, which were recorded to last twenty years. This was worn with a coat of a distinctive New England cut and color. A man's coat often reflected his station in life, and the styles of coats varied greatly. They were often dyed with the barks of the forest, and ranged in color from a gentlemanly black, to a common man's brown sumac, to a gaudy orange or purple. A waistcoat, a pair of breeches or long trousers with wool stockings, and leather shoes rounded out the typical clothing of a member of the Rhode Island Militia. The clothing was made almost exclusively at home out of materials at hand. Much of the clothing was passed down through the generations, and was often recycled into other garments.[5]

Rhode Island never adopted any law creating guidelines for the outfitting of the state militia, except that the captain of each company was to make sure each man would have a musket and bayonet.[6] In 1775, Massachusetts created the following guidelines for its militia:

> A good firearm with a steel or iron ramrod…a bayonet fitted to his gun, a scabbard and belt therfor, and a cutting sword, or a tomahawk or hatchet, a pouch containing a cartridge box that would hold fifteen rounds of cartridges at least, six flints, one pound of powder, forty leaden ball fitten to his gun, a knapsack and blanket, a canteen or wooden bottle sufficient to hold one quart.[7]

Officers in Rhode Island would have endeavored to equip their men like this, but few of the men in Scituate met the Massachusetts guidelines.

The firearms of the militia often varied as much as their clothing. The majority of the men carried a piece known as a fowler. This weapon was often a thrift piece, made out of spare parts from other muskets, to create an effective hunting weapon.

The fowler was a weapon well suited for the type of woodland skirmishing fought on April 19. The piece was often loaded with a large ball and buckshot, creating a deadly effect at close range. The fowler was stocked to the muzzle, and could not accept a bayonet, making it ineffective for the type of linear warfare often fought during the Revolution.[8] Some of the men were equipped with either a .69 caliber Charleville, or a .75 caliber Long Land Pattern musket. These were military pieces carried home from the French and Indian War. In October 1774, the Colony of Rhode Island captured Fort George in Newport Harbor, and took into custody two thousand Long Land Pattern muskets, and stands of arms consisting of a belt, cartridge box, and bayonet. These weapons were distributed to the towns in Rhode Island as a common stock, held in reserve for those men who needed arms, but did not have any. Men who did not have any weapons could purchase them for £20. Scituate received two hundred of these weapons.[9]

The flintlock musket was loaded with powder and a round ball. In military service both powder and ball were carried in pre-measured paper cartridges. Cartridge boxes were rarely seen in militia service, except when either made at home, or captured on the battlefield. The ones made at home often consisted of no more then a wooden block, drilled with holes to hold the cartridges. This was covered by a leather flap. Instead the majority of the New England militia carried a powder horn. These were made of cow or ox horn, and could hold a pound of powder. The horns were ornately carved with such designs as coats of arms, patriotic slogans, and maps. These horns were often passed down through the generations. In the 1890s one of Captain Joseph Knight's descendents described his powder horn as being "the largest one I have ever saw."[10] Those without a cartridge box often used a shot pouch: a small leather bag in which spare flints, musket tools, musket balls, and buckshot were carried.

In addition to a musket, most militiamen also carried a cutting tool, usually either a tomahawk or sword. A knapsack or woolen blanket was utilized to carry personnel nessaceries such as a spare pair of socks, or an extra shirt. A wooden canteen held water, while a small linen bag held simple rations of meat, bread, and cheese.[11]

Captain Joseph Knight: A recreation of how Captain Joseph Knight
might have appeared on April 20, 1775. He wears a round hat, which is
cockaded to show he is a member of the militia. He also wears a green
New England Coat, a brown waistcoat, and breeches, as well as farmer's
boots. He is armed with a long barreled New England fowler, and a short
sword. He carries a homemade cartridge box, and canteen, as well as an
imported English blanket. Photograph by author.

The field equipment of the militia also represented one key aspect about them: practicality. Every item they carried had a purpose. The utensils the men carried were the same that were used at their table each night. Officers and men dressed and looked the same. It was common for men to call officers by their first name, and be very close to them, something unheard of in other armies at the time. Militia officers did not lead their men, as much as they gave them suggestions on what to do. Oftentimes an order was debated, in a town meeting style, and could be voted upon whether or not to be obeyed. This often led to confusion, but during battle, officers' orders were obeyed without question.

Thus armed, equipped, and drilled, the Scituate Militia took to the field. Though often gawked at by the British Regular for their dress and drill, the militia would prove to be of invaluable service during the conflict ahead. In Rhode Island the Scituate Militia would be in the thick of it all.

CHAPTER FOUR

Preparations

In December 1773, the Boston Sons of Liberty threw 394 chests of tea into Boston Harbor. This was simply the latest act in a series of events leading to armed rebellion. In response to the Tea Party the British Parliament passed the Coercive Acts. In June of 1774, in an attempt to stop further acts of rebellion, Boston Harbor was closed.

In response to this action, a town meeting was called in Scituate on September 26, 1774, at the Angell Tavern. The opening of the proceedings during the meeting read:

> Having taken into consideration the dark and gloomy clouds that seem to threaten a total destruction of the liberties of this, our Native country, in general, the distressing circumstances of the town of Boston in particular; their harbor blockaded; the inhabitants cut from all trade and commerce of the sea.[1]

Also voted during the meeting was for Lieutenant Colonel Ezekiel Cornell to collect "fat sheep" for the relief of the people of Boston. In November, Lieutenant Colonel Cornell delivered 120 sheep to Boston. In March 1775, the people of Boston sent a letter of thanks to the people of Scituate for the sheep.[2]

In October 1774, a young man in a madder red coat arrived in the woods of western Scituate, claiming he was a deserter from the British Army in Boston. His name was William Boswell. He claimed that he had deserted for burning some bread, and feared the punishment. After being captured, Boswell escaped and made his way to Scituate.[3]

Throughout the winter of 1774-1775 the Scituate Militia drilled frequently, as often as twice a week for the seventy-six officers and men in Captain Joseph Knight's Second Company of

Minutemen. Eight of Knight's kinsmen were in this company. On January 16, 1775, the company mustered for a day of drill at the new home of Lieutenant Samuel Wilbur, a lad of seventeen years, who was Captain Knight's second in command.[4]

The majority of the men enjoyed training day, as it provided an opportunity to socialize, drink, and be paid two shillings. Some of the men, did not share their officers' sense of duty. Many fines were levied against men for not going to the training field, or not arriving with the proper equipment. This can clearly be seen in a letter that Captain Joseph Knight wrote to his brother, Robert on April 11, 1775:

> Providence to Robert Knight, Clerk of the First Military Company in the Town of Scituate & County of Providence. Greeting- Whereas David Yaw, Nathaniel Phillips, & John Manchester all Soldiers born upon the Trained Band List of Enlisted Soldiers in the said Company. Were Legally warned on the third Day of Febuary the Company by the Commanding officer of the day. While under arms at the head of Company to appear at the House of Captain Andrew Angells inholder- on Friday the third Day of March at Nine of the Clock in the Forenoon Compleat in arms as the Law directs in- order to be instructed in Military Disipline yet they all Neglete and wholly refused to appear and have not made any Such excuse as the Law Decriets. Whereby Each of them have Incurred the Penalty of three Shillings Lawful money and have not paid the same or any part there of- these are therefore in His Majesties name to Require you forthwith to Collect the aforesaid Sums of three Schillings Each of the said David, Nathaniel, & John and upon repeal to pay the Same that then of the Personel Estate of the said David, Nathaniel, & John you do Forthwith Levey by Distraint the aforesaid Sums to geather with the four pence Each for Distraining and the same to Expose to Sail at Publick Vandue as he Law Directs and out of the money arising out of such sale you are to pay the aforesaid Sums into the town treasury of S. town after deducting for your trouble twelve and one half percent the over plus if any there bee to be Returned to the owners and for Want of Sufficient Estate goods & Chattles to be by you found to

Satisfy as aforesaid that then you Committ the said David, Nathaniel, & John to His Majesties Gaol in Said County there to remain until Said Sums to be paid for which this Warrant- Shall be your Sufficient Discharge and make Return to my self how you execute this Warrant within twenty days from this date fail not Given under my hand & Seal in Scituate this Eleventh day of April in the fifteenth year of his Said Majestys Reign George the Third King of Great-Britain && AD 1775

Joseph Knight, Capt[5]

The fines collected were used to help pay the bounties to the minutemen, as well as to provide powder for training. A firing range and gun workshop were established in Rockland, making different caliber bullets for the men's muskets. Supplies were at a bare minimum and many towns were unable to supply their men with powder and balls to train with. Scituate men trained often and it would prove important in years ahead. The training would continue until the outbreak of hostilities.[6]

In February 1775, a young doctor named Caleb Fisk moved to South Scituate from Cranston. He quickly set up a small practice, and joined the Second Company of Minutemen as a surgeon. Fisk would later become part of the staff of the Third Providence County Regiment. He was described as "Scituate's richest man."[7]

In early April 1775, the Colony of Rhode Island distributed the arms captured from Fort George. They also distributed lead, powder, and flints to the towns. Scituate received ninety pounds of powder, 143 pounds of lead, and 572 flints. These were held with the muskets at the common stock at the Angell Tavern, however the lead was distributed to the men by the officers so they could cast their own bullets.[8] With these preparations Scituate was ready for the coming conflict.

On the night of April 18, 1775, a column of eight hundred British Grenadiers and Light Infantrymen marched west into the cool night of a New England spring. At 5:00 on the morning of the nineteenth they arrived in the quiet village of Lexington, Massachusetts. After a standoff that appeared to last for hours a shot ran out in the early morning dawn from behind the Buckman Tavern. The British Light Infantry returned fire with a sharp volley, killing or wounding seventeen Americans. Later that morning the two sides would again meet at a small wooden bridge north of Concord, Massachusetts. As Americans began to fall, the cry was given. "Fire fellow soldiers, for God sakes. Fire" The American Revolution began. Immediately riders were sent throughout New England to rally additional militia support. One of these riders rode to Rhode Island. Men from Scituate would be the first to respond.

CHAPTER FIVE

The Call to Arms

R hode Island received news of the Battles of Lexington and Concord by a letter in the late afternoon of April 19, 1775. Almost immediately a rider was sent down the Plainfield Pike to notify the countryside of the event. Around 6:00 p.m. the rider approached Scituate yelling, "They're Fighting, They're Fighting!" The Revolution had come to Scituate.[1]

Benjamin Boss, an eighteen-year-old farmer from South Scituate was in a swamp near his house cutting beanpoles for the spring planting. Boss threw down his axe, picked up his musket and mounted his horse, and started on the road to Boston. Late that night Boss would meet his good friend, David Burlingame, of Gloucester. Together they would serve throughout the war.[2]

Captain Joseph Knight was also in his fields, "sowing oats." He immediately stopped, and mustered the Second Company of Minutemen at the Angell Tavern. Fifty-two men responded to the call. During the night of the nineteenth the men sat in the tavern's taproom and decided on a course of action. The next morning they would march to Boston. On the morning of April 20, 1775, the men formed a line to sign the muster roll; the roll was headed with these words:

> We do hereby enlist ourselves as volunteers in the present Emergency in defense of our Country and rights of Privileges and Liberty.

The men who signed the roll were Joseph Knight, captain; Samuel Wilbur (lieutenant), Benjamin Wood, Isaac Horton, John Hill, Nathan Walker, James Parker, John Bennet, Jr., Jeremiah Almy, Joseph Remington, Nathan Ralfe (ensign), John I. Kilton, Jonathan Knight, Jr., Joseph Briggs, David Knight, Joseph Collins, William Taylor, John Manchester, Edward Bennett, Thomas

Parker, John Edwards, Jr., Simeon Wilbur (sergeant), Isaiah Austin, Samuel Eldridge, Christopher Knight, Samuel Hopkins, Benajah Bosworth, Obadiah Ralfe, Ezekiel Wood, Caleb Fisk, doctor, John Phillips (drummer), Constant Graves, Stukely Thornton, James Andrews, Jr., Christopher Collins, Joseph Bennet, Thomas Knight, Peleg Colvin, Eleazor Westcott, Caleb Steere, Collins Roberts, Daniel Fisk, William Knight, Nathan Franklin, Uriah Franklin, Jr., Ephriam Edwards, Stephen Edwards, Francis Fuller, Jr., Benjamin Whitmore, William Stafford, Daniel Angell, Furmer Tanner.

After signing the roll, they began their march to Boston. On April 22, somewhere in Massachusetts, the company was intercepted by riders from Lexington who told Captain Knight and his men to return to Rhode Island, as more men were available than supplies could provide for. Most of the company turned back, but thirteen men continued to march to Boston. Captain Knight's Second Company of Minutemen has the honor of being the first Rhode Islanders to join in the Revolution.[3]

In May 1775, the Rhode Island General Assembly voted to raise an Army of Observation to join the Grand American Army around Boston. The army would consist of 1500 men in three infantry regiments, and a battery of artillery, commanded by Brigadier General Nathanael Greene of Coventry. Each private upon enlisting would be given a blanket and a knapsack, in addition to forty shillings per month. The men were also given a bounty of forty shillings if they brought their own muskets and cartridge boxes.[4]

The men of Scituate were quick to join the Army of Observation, filling up two whole companies in the Second Rhode Island Regiment commanded by Colonel Daniel Hitchcock of Providence. Captain Stephen Kimball of North Scituate, and Captain Jeremiah Olney of Smithfield commanded the Scituate companies. Among the men in Captain Kimball's company was Benjamin Boss, who had left Scituate on April 19. In Captain Olney's company were the thirteen men of Captain Knight's Company who had continued to march to Boston. They were Corporal Benjamin Wood, Drummer John Phillips, and Privates John Manchester, Collins Roberts, Joseph Collins, Samuel Eldrich, Stephen Edwards, Caleb Steere, Joseph Bennet, Stuckley

Thornton, Christopher Collins, and Edward Bennet. On June 17, 1775 the Battle of Bunkers Hill was fought. The Rhode Island Brigade was not engaged, instead remaining in their camp at Roxbury. With the battle raging, dispatch riders were again sent throughout New England to rally additional militia support incase the British broke through the American defenses into the Massachusetts countryside. When the news reached Providence, 1,000 men were quickly on their way to Boston, including a company of Scituate men under Captain Joseph Knight. After spending several days in Boston and with the British threat subsided, the Rhode Island Militia returned to their homes.[5]

The men in the Grand American Army held the British in check around Boston during the summer of 1775. In September; Colonel Benedict Arnold of Connecticut proposed an invasion of Canada to capture Quebec. Among the companies formed, three were made up solely of Rhode Islanders. Three Scituate men volunteered, and became part of the company commanded by Captain Simeon Thayer. They were Sergeant Samuel Singleton, Corporal Moses Cocran, and Private Abram Jones. Jones was discharged before the march began, but Corporal Cocran and Sergeant Singleton participated in the expedition and were never seen again. They died in the woods of Maine, as many did during the march. Quebec was not taken, and many of the officers and men, including all of the Rhode Islanders, were captured.[6]

During the summer of 1775 in Scituate a large beacon was established upon Chopmist Hill. The beacon consisted of a bucket of tar suspended from the top of an eighty-foot pole. The plan was that if the British invaded Rhode Island, the militia would see the beacon, and muster. The beacon could be seen as far away as Norwich, Connecticut. It was maintained by Squire Williams, who spent eight years living in a hut on Chopmist Hill. A guard, consisting of a lieutenant, corporal, and twelve privates, was also posted at the Scituate Beacon. They were drawn from the Third Providence County Regiment, and were rotated frequently. The beacon never lit, except for in July 1780 as a sign that the French had finally arrived. [7]

A woodcut of the Scituate Beacon, located on Chopmist Hill.
Field, *Defenses.*

CHAPTER SIX

Defending the Bay

W ith the outbreak of open conflict, many of the officers and men in the Third Providence County Regiment joined the Continental Army, or the Rhode Island State Brigade. This brigade was designed to be kept in the state, but would soon be sent to help the Continentals in New York. Brigade commander Brigadier General Christopher Lippitt became colonel of the First Rhode Island State Regiment. Colonel William West was promoted to brigadier general. Lieutenant Colonel Ezekiel Cornell became lieutenant colonel of the Second Rhode Island Regiment. Major John Colwell was promoted to lieutenant colonel of the Third Providence County Regiment.[1]

In December of 1775, General William Howe, the British commander in Boston, decided to send several regiments to capture Newport, and then Providence. The plan was discovered, and Rhode Island Governor Nicholas Cooke sent the following message to Captain Joseph Knight on December 19:

> You are hereby directed to gather together the company under your command with all possible expedition and march them to this town in order to be transported to Rhode Island for the defense of that island. You are to be careful that the men are properly equipped with arms, ammunition and blankets fit for immediate service. I have advice from Gen. Washington that eight large transports, with two tenders, having on board one regiment of foot, and three companies of horse sailed from Boston last Saturday, and I have no doubt that your officers and men will exert themselves upon this occasion with their usual ardor.

Captain Knight quickly mustered his company and marched the seven miles to Providence, to reinforce the fort on Field's Point.

When the Regulars saw the reinforced garrison, they returned to Boston.[2]

From Providence, Captain Knight took a detachment of his company to Warwick Neck, where Brigadier General West now commanded. Here was built a large earthwork and battery. Across Narragansett Bay from Warwick Neck was Prudence Island. Here was kept a stock of sheep for the Colony. The task of the troops on Warwick Neck was to protect the west passage of Narragansett Bay, as well as the sheep on Prudence. The starving British soldiers in Boston desperately needed fresh meat, so in late December 1775, Vice Admiral Richard Graves dispatched Captain James Wallace to Narragansett Bay to forage for supplies.[3]

It was long thought the British would attack Prudence. On January 11, 1776, exiled Tory Governor Joseph Wanton wrote to Captain Samuel Pearce, the commander of the Prudence Island Boys, that on January 12, Captain Wallace would stop on Prudence to purchase "stock and provisions at the highest price." Captain Pearce immediately wrote back to Wanton exclaiming that he and his men would be waiting for Wallace with their bayonets. Captain Pearce then ordered all of the women and children off of Prudence, and as many sheep as possible. Then he wrote to Brigadier General West at Warwick, requesting reinforcements.[4]

General West was quick to respond, and in the early morning hours of January 12, sent the following message to Captain Joseph Knight:

> You are herby ordered to take a scow down to the Pearl and report upon fatigue duty to Prudence with nine privates with a commission officer and serjeant or corporal.

Captain Knight mustered his men, and they rowed the half-mile to Prudence in a whaleboat. The Scituate men who Captain Knight took with him were Sergeants William Brownell and Simeon Wilbur; Corporal Abraham Angell, and Joseph Turner, Stephen Leach, Oliver Leach, Oliver Fisk, Zebedee Snow, Christopher Edwards, Joseph Wight, Moses Colvin, and Christopher Knight. Once arriving on Prudence, the Scituate men joined the Prudence Island Boys in the marshes at the southern end of the island and waited for Wallace.[5]

At 4:00 in the afternoon of January 12, described as "a fateful cold day," Captain Wallace landed 250 British Marines and sailors to forage for supplies. They landed and quickly captured one hundred sheep. They were met by Captain Knight and the Prudence Island Militia, who fired several volleys and quickly retreated to the northern end of the island. After being pursued by the British they decided to be prudent and leave the island for the night. They then retired back to Warwick Neck. That night it was thought that Wallace would return to complete his task the following morning. As such the following day the men returned to Prudence. This time they were reinforced by eighty men from Bristol. In addition fifty men from Captain Knights Company arrived at Warwick, and were ready to launch if needed. As thought Captain Wallace returned the next morning and carried off some hay. During this action, a British foraging party met a militia ambush, in which five British Sailors became casualties. Captain Wallace leaves the best description of the action in his report to Vice Admiral Graves:

Rose, Rhode Island 14 January 1776

The Rebels having for some time past kept from one to two hundred Men upon the Islands to prevent our supplies- And by a Law making it Death for any one to supply us to a great inconvenience being much in want of Hay- On Friday morning the 12th instant I stood up the Bay with H.M. ships Glasgow, Swan, and Tenders in Order to procure some- At about 12 at Noon being abreast of Prudence we saw a body of Armed Men with a field piece, who followed us as we sailed along- At the South end of the Island I saw a quantity of Hay, and determined to land and seize it- This they perceived and set fire to the Stacks and retired to their Stone fences to oppose us (every field has stone enclosures) We landed, beat them from Fence to Fence for four Miles into their Country, firing and wasting the Country as we advanced along; We burnt twelve of fifteen Farm Houses, took a great deal of stock, when Night coming on we gave over the pursuit, and retired back to our boats, the people was fatigues and Cold, and fearing they might be Frost bit Ordered them to embark and leave the Cattle off, but,

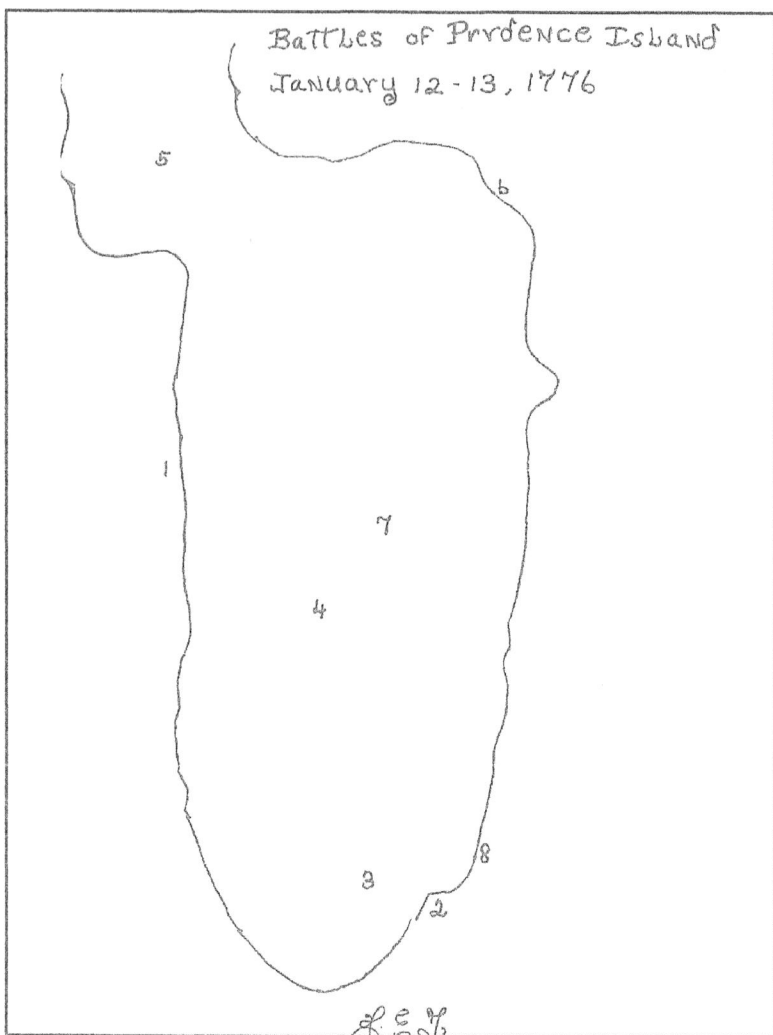

Map by Joyce Knight Townsend

1. Scituate Militia arrive from Warwick
2. Captain Wallace Lands
3. Prudence Island Boys, and Scituate Militia exchange volleys
   with British Marines
4. Militia retreat up Prudence, exchanging fire with British Forces
5. Militia retires to this point
6. Bristol Militia land
7. Ambush of British Foraging Party
8. Captain Wallace Retires.

during the night, reinforcements of Five or Six hundred Men had been sent on and drove the Cattle to the other extremity of the island, And large Bodies of Armed Rebels stood behind Stone fences to oppose us In this situation we contended ourselves with taking off some Hay Stacks in their sight and Embarked our men again- In the attack the first day we killed two of their men, and took two prisoners both Wounded- The next day some of the Swans and Glasgows Men staying too far from the Main Body fell into an Ambush, and one man of the Swan was killed, two Mortally Wounded, and one Slightly,- One man of the Glasgow was shot thro' the thigh and fell into the hands of the Rebels, and one slightly wounded- Our loss wo'd been less, had our people have had less spirit.[6]

British casualties during the two days of fighting were three killed, two wounded, and one captured. Also wounded was a Royal Navy lieutenant who was rescued by British Marines. Militia casualties were two killed and two wounded. One of the killed and one of the wounded were Scituate Minutemen; their identity has never been known. After the Battles for Prudence Island, Captain Wallace remained in Narragansett Bay for several more days, collecting wood, forage, and sheep from Hope and Patience Islands, and then he returned to Boston. It was not enough to support the British, for on March 17, 1776, Boston was evacuated.

For his gallantry during the Battles of Prudence Island, Captain Joseph Knight was promoted to major in the Third Providence County Regiment. Major Knight's brother, Jonathan, became captain of the Second Company of Minutemen, while eighteen-year-old Samuel Wilbur became captain of the Fifth Company of Militia.[7] With many Scituate men serving in the Continental Army, the militia companies were reorganized, and new boundaries were drawn up. On February 5, 1776, Captain Jonathan Knight added the following names to the Second Company of Minutemen: Daniel Dexter, Peter Pierce, Alexander Lovell, Ebenezer Handy, Joseph Turner, John Gunnison, Isaiah Ashton, Benjain Bacon, Nathan Matthewson, Christopher Edwards, Knight Wilbur, Abraham Angell, and Moses Colvin.[8]

The Second Company of Minutemen returned to Scituate in March 1776, and was relieved at Warwick by the Third Company. The companies rotated duty at Warwick Neck every fifteen days, in order of the company number. Lieutenant Colonel John Colwell and Major Knight also alternated duty at Warwick, so one would always be in Scituate, while the other was on duty at the Neck.[9]

With the British forces driven out of Boston, Washington moved his army out of Boston to New York. His route through Rhode Island carried him through Scituate, along the Plainfield Pike. Accompanying the Continental Army were several newly cast Hope Furnace cannon. Immediately after the British landed upon Long Island, things began to go very poorly for the Continentals. The only relief appeared to be on July 9, 1776, when the Declaration of Independence was first read to the men. Amongst the signers was Stephen Hopkins, a native of Scituate. The only American victory of the campaign occurred on September 16, 1776, at the Battle of Harlem Heights. During the engagement, Lieutenant Colonel Cornell led the Second Rhode Island in a successful flank attack, and received much praise from Major General Nathanael Greene. After losing several more engagements, the Continentals were driven out of New York and pursued into New Jersey and Pennsylvania. The war appeared to be all but over.[10]

On December 26, 1776, Washington won a stunning victory against a Hessian garrison at Trenton, New Jersey. Though the Second Rhode Island Regiment was not engaged, the men quickly arrived to share in the plunder; a barefoot Benjamin Boss recorded the capture of the finest pair of Hessian boots in the city. On January 2, 1777, the Crown counterattacked at the Second Battle of Trenton. At this battle the Second Rhode Island was assigned as the rearguard to the Continental Army as they made their way to Princeton to attack a British garrison. General Washington himself assigned sixty-two men from the two Scituate companies along with two Hope Furnace cannon to guard the Assinpink Bridge. On a high bluff overlooking the bridge the Scituate men built a small fortification, deployed, and waited. From their position they could cover the approaches to the bridge, and the bridge itself. For two hours in total darkness the men of Scituate held firm against constant assaults by the Hessian Grenadiers and British Light

Infantry, inflicting severe casualties. Benjamin Boss wrote home to his parents in Scituate, claiming, "the creek flowed red with British blood." The men of Scituate stood and lost two men killed. Their stand allowed Washington to slip behind the Crown Army, and make it onto Princeton. At this engagement the Second Rhode Island again played a prominent role in helping to defeat the British garrison.[11]

These victories came at a crucial time. They encouraged the American people to continue to support the Revolution, and for the men to reenlist to continue their fight for freedom. The people of Scituate were in good spirits as a new year came. However, the Revolution was soon going to come to Rhode Island's doorstep.

Second Battle of Trenton: An early woodcut of the Second Battle of Trenton, showing the two companies of Scituate men in the Second Rhode Island Regiment, and their two Hope Furnace cannon successfully defending the Assinpink Bridge from constant attacks by the Crown Forces. Robert Edwin Walker, *History of Trenton*.

CHAPTER SEVEN

Invasion

On the morning of December 8, 1776, the citizens of Newport, Rhode Island, awoke to find their island invaded by a large Crown Force commanded by Major General Henry Clinton. Stationed on the island was a small force commanded by Brigadier General West. As the British made their way onto the island, he and his men made a hasty retreat back to Warwick. Almost immediately after the invasion the Rhode Island Militia sprang into action to contain the British and Hessian forces upon Rhode Island, by setting up many forts and batteries to protect the shore and Providence. The militia launched constant nighttime raids to gather intelligence, and in July 1777 captured Major General Richard Prescott from his bed in Portsmouth.[1]

The Scituate Militia also was quick to respond by sending detachments to Warwick, Providence, Bristol, and Tiverton. The militia companies were each rotated, along Narragansett Bay. Here the men would spend thirty days on duty, would be relieved, and would again go on duty two months later. In this manner, at least two companies in the Third Providence County Regiment were always on duty.[2]

During this time the officers made sure that their men were well equipped with such items as muskets, bayonets, blankets, cartridge boxes, and snapsacks. Captains Jonathan Knight, and Samuel Wilbur, and General West were constantly writing returns for equipment, mostly made by the women of Scituate. Also at this time, Dr. Caleb Fisk was occupied examining the men, and writing discharges for those who had suffered the effects of a military campaign, such as dysentery, smallpox, and malnutrition. For coastwatching duty, the men were paid large amounts of money. For one month's service, a field officer was paid £18, a captain £12, lieutenant £8, ensign £6, sergeant £3, and a private £2, a huge

16 guns 16 Cartdge Boxes
12 Blankitt 3 Snap cacks
July y⁹ day 1777 then Reciued
the above guns Cartudg Boxes Blankit
Snapt Sacks of Cap⁹ Joseph Kimble and
orders Being the property of the toue
of Sulmate J day Reciued By yo
W.m West

Return of equipage. One of many receipts signed by officers of the
Third Providence County Regiment for supplies received by them
from the town. This one was signed by General West at Warwick in
1777. Author's collection.

sum for a common farmer or laborer. These large wages would have dire consequences.[3]

On April 28, 1777 one of the most important town meetings held during the Revolution was called forth at the Angell Tavern. Amongst the measures discussed, Scituate wanted to bring forth legislation in the Rhode Island General Assembly which would increase the number of seats that the town held. Despite a large number of residents, Scituate was only limited to two seats by the Royal Charter of 1683. This was the first time since the inception of the state, that the original charter had been questioned; it would prove very similar to measures proposed in the 1840s by Thomas Dorr. The measure passed, and soon Scituate received three additional seats in the General Assembly. The second issue discussed was the militia wages. The officers of the Third Providence County Regiment were given wages for their time served, beyond that paid to them by the state to make up for their work missed at home. However the soldiers did not, which led to a very low morale in the Regiment. As such the Town Council, which included a large amount of officers, voted to decrease the officers' wages by one half, and to give the wages to the men, without increasing the tax burden upon the town. As such the men's wages rose, and the officers' decreased, thus creating a great increase in the morale of the Regiment, despite the fact that the Continental script they were paid in was near worthless. The third measure adopted was to hold one-fourth of the battalion in readiness at all times to instantly march at any point needed, within Rhode Island or not. Also at this time, the town had a large speculation in a salt works near Pawtuxet, producing valuable salt for the town, which was desperately needed to preserve food for the soldiers. It took half a cord of wood to purchase one bushel of salt. Accordingly the boys of Scituate were occupied chopping wood to trade for the salt, which was used by all in the town, and was a very valuable commodity.[4]

With little to do during their month-long coastwatching details, and with Crown Forces safely penned up in Newport, the men had little to do in camp. Soon gambling became a constant problem, and low prices on alcohol led to a large amount of the men becoming intoxicated while on duty. Coastwatching duty was not always so monotonous. On November 30, 1777, a group of

Scituate men were attacked by a fatigue party of British soldiers in Kingstown. Private Oliver Fisk of the First Company was captured and taken to Newport, and thence was transported to New York. On May 30, 1778, he died aboard the prison ship *Good Intent*.[5]

In March 1777, Stephen Kimball, a veteran of two years of hard campaigning through New York, New Jersey, and Pennsylvania returned to Scituate in a worn-out condition. He was placed in command of the Alarm List, which was composed of old men and invalids still able to bear arms. Their task was to defend Scituate when the militia was away. At this same time Lieutenant Colonel Ezekiel Cornell was discharged from Continental service, and returned to Rhode Island. He was promoted to Brigadier General, and given command of the Rhode Island State Brigade. Lieutenant Colonel John Colwell was on duty in Providence, leaving Major Joseph Knight in command of the Third Providence County Regiment.[6]

During the summer of 1777, an invasion of the island of Rhode Island was planned. But due to a lack of forces, with Continental and Militia units fighting John Burgoyne's Army in New York, and Sir William Howe's Army in Pennsylvania. As well as poor planning upon the part of American commander Major General John Spencer, nicknamed "Granny" by his men, the invasion was postponed. In preparation of the campaign General West's brigade was reorganized. The First Regiment was to be left behind to protect Providence. The Brigade now contained the Second Providence County Regiment, commanded by Colonel Chad Brown, and the Third Providence County Regiment under Major Knight.[7] Also during the summer of 1777, several changes were taking place amongst the companies in the regiments. The Rhode Island General Assembly had voted to disband the minutemen. As such the First Company of Minutemen reverted to the Third Company, and the Second Company of Minutemen again became the First Company.[8]

On October 17, 1777, Lieutenant General John Burgoyne surrendered the British Northern Army at Saratoga, New York. This event was news throughout the western world; it was the first time an entire British Army had ever surrendered. This prompted the French and other nations to aid the American cause. The

American people rejoiced at the news of French support. From
now on they would not be alone in their struggle for independence

The home of Joseph Knight, built in the 1730s. Members of the Knight family continued to live in it until the house was condemned by Providence for the Scituate Reservoir in 1920. Author's Collection.

CHAPTER EIGHT

Home

With over seven hundred Scituate men serving in both the Continental Army and the militia, the people who stayed behind rushed to support the Revolution. In June 1776, all of the men in the town were required to take an Oath of Allegiance to the Colony of Rhode Island. Those not taking the oath were promptly expelled from the town. Later in September, all of the men signed the Declaration of Independence; pledging themselves to their new nation.[1]

Prior to the Rhode Island Regiments leaving Rhode Island in 1777, all of the men were inoculated against the smallpox, and two houses in North Scituate were taken over for the task. On November 15, 1777, Captain Jonathan Kimball was appointed to supply the families of the men in the Continental Army with food and money to see them through the winter.[2] During the winter of 1777-1778, while the men of the Second Rhode Island Regiment were freezing at Valley Forge, Brigadier General William West was appointed the head of a committee to collect blankets for the Continentals. Thirteen were collected and delivered to Scituate men at Valley Forge. Hope Furnace was also occupied casting pots and kettles for both the Continentals and the militia.[3]

The women of Scituate also performed an important part in the Revolution. Many ran the family farms and took over the important task of raising sheep to provide wool for the soldiers. They also sewed many linen shirts, and knitted wool stockings. Elizabeth Knight, the wife of Major Joseph Knight wrote her husband the following letter while he was at Warwick in 1777:

> These lines are to let you know that we are all well at present. I want you to come home soon as you can, to see about getting some flax, for it is very scarce to be had.

The Great House: The home of William West on the
Danielson Pike. Author's Collection.

There are some men who want to be boarded at your house, and I want you to send to me whether you are willing to board them or not. So I remain your loving wife, Elizabeth Knight.[4]

Brigadier General West was also contributing to the welfare of the town. In 1761 he purchased five hundred acres of woodlands on the Danielson Pike. In 1775 he erected the "Great House," a large clapboard farmhouse, on his land. This was the largest house ever built in Scituate. While General West was away at war, his farm continued to function, and produced large amounts of cheese for the men in his brigade.[5]

The Angell Tavern also prospered during the Revolution, serving food and drink to many weary soldiers as they traveled the Plainfield Pike.[6] Despite a large number of its citizens at war, Scituate remained a very active place during the Revolution. Amongst the most active places in the State of Rhode Island was the Hope Furnace.

CHAPTER NINE

Hope Furnace

In 1765, a bed of iron ore was discovered in Western Cranston. That same year, Stephen Hopkins built an iron furnace on the Pawtuxet River in the village of Hope. Hopkins then created and began selling shares in the Hope Furnace Company, and by 1766 the furnace was in full production, casting anchors, iron fencing, nails, and bar iron for use in making steel. The furnace consisted of a twenty-foot tower, with a hole on the top. Wood was stoked into it from the bottom, while the iron and limestone was inserted through the hole. The iron and limestone melted together, and was then drawn off as steel, and poured into the various molds to create the finished product. The cannon were cast solid, and were bored out using a water powered drill. Joseph Knight bought several shares in the company, and used his horses to carry iron and wood to the furnace. At this time, Hopkins appointed his son Rufus as the superintendent of the furnace.[1]

In 1774, Hope Furnace began to cast cannon for privateers. In 1775 the Rhode Island General Assembly ordered twenty-seven cannon to be erected at strategic points along Narragansett Bay. Hope Furnace was quick to respond, and soon began to cast two cannon a day, and proofed them on a bluff overlooking the Pawtuxet River. These cannon were erected as follows.

Jamestown: Three twelve-pounders
South Kingstown: Two eighteen-pounders and two nine-
    pounders
Warwick Neck: Two eighteen-pounders
Field's Point: Five nine-pounders
Warren: Two nine-pounders
Bristol: Seven nine-pounders
Tiverton: Four nine-pounders[2]

Proof Mark: All products made at Hope Furnace carried this distinctive "HF" marking. Photograph by author.

Hope Furnace Cannon: A six pounder Hope Furnace cannon, used during the Revolution by the Third Providence County Regiment. This is the sole surviving Hope Furnace cannon. Photograph by author.

In 1776, the Continental Congress asked Hope Furnace to produce as many cannon as possible, and soon the furnace was producing cannon ranging from four-pound field guns, to twenty-four-pound siege cannon, as well as different types of cannon ammunition, such as solid shot, grape, and canister. Each cannon and piece of ammunition was stamped with a distinctive "HF" mark for Hope Furnace. The furnace employed over one hundred skilled workers. Men employed at Hope Furnace were exempt from militia duty, which always left the Seventh Company severely undermanned.

Cannon were sold as a pair: four-pound cannon sold for £550 per pair, and six-pound cannon sold for £1050 per pair. Ten Hope Furnace twenty-four-pounders were also shipped to the Main Army under Washington for use as siege weapons. These cannon were used during the Siege of Yorktown. When Washington fired the first shot into Yorktown, it was from a Hope Furnace cannon. In 1781, Hope Furnace cast four light six-pounders to create an artillery battery in the Third Providence County Regiment; these guns followed the regiment wherever it went. In addition to casting cannon for the Continental Army, the furnace also cast cannon for New England privateers, especially those sailing out of Salem, Massachusetts.[3]

After the signing of the Treaty of Paris, Hope Furnace went back to casting pots and anchors. Cannon making resumed in 1794 for the United States Navy, and continued until 1814, when the iron source ran out. Hope Furnace ran into debt, and was forced to close. Soon the forest would reclaim the furnace and its grounds. Most of the Hope Furnace cannon were melted down for scrap to help pay off the debts. Although it was only in operation for a short time, Hope Furnace produced cannon that served in every engagement of the war, and contributed much to victory.[4]

The Continentals

In early 1777, the American Revolution was at a low point. The British had captured Newport and still held New York, and were poised to capture Albany and Philadelphia. Washington's Main Army had been reduced from 25,000 to 3,000 men, and only after the victories at Trenton and Princeton did more men rush to the Continental cause. In February, the enlistments of the whole army, including the Second Rhode Island Regiment ran out. A new army needed to be raised quickly.

In January, the Rhode Island General Assembly voted to raise two regiments for the Continental Army, the First and Second Rhode Island Regiments. The First was to be recruited in Kent and Kings County, while the Second would be raised in Providence County. Colonel Christopher Greene of Warwick, recently released from prison in Quebec, was given command of the First. Command of the Second was given to Colonel Israel Angell, of Johnston, who replaced Colonel Daniel Hitchcock, who died at Princeton. Jeremiah Olney, who had led a Scituate Company in the Army of Observation, was commissioned Lieutenant Colonel of the Second Rhode Island.[1]

Recruiting for the two regiments was extremely slow, partially due to the fact that they would be enlisting for three years, rather than one. By May, only six hundred men had been raised, and the two regiments were each assigned around three hundred men. With the British blockading Narragansett Bay, many sailors joined the Rhode Island Regiments, including a large proportion of foreigners. A recruiting office was established at Rhode Island College in Providence. It was here that many men enlisted. Upon enlistment the men were issued their regimental clothing, consisting of a brown coat, faced with red, as well as brown waistcoat and breeches. The men were also issued with their firelocks, which were the remainder of those captured from Fort George. In response to General Washington's orders there barrels were shortened four inches. With recruiting going slowly in Providence, the captains were dispatched throughout Rhode Island in search of men. Captain Sylvanus Shaw was assigned to recruit in Scituate and Coventry. Amongst the men he enlisted was Benjamin Boss, who had previously served two years in the Continental Line. In recognition of his past service he was promoted to sergeant. Another member of the company was Joseph Angell, of South Scituate. He was described as a "crack shot." In addition many Scituate men joined Captain Stephen Olney's Company which was recruited from Smithfield.[2]

Despite being well short of their required strength, the two Rhode Island Regiments were ordered to join the Continental Army, which was encamped at Peekskill, New York. The two regiments marched down the familiar Plainfield Pike and arrived at Peekskill fifteen days later. Here they were assigned to Varnum's Rhode Island Brigade, consisting of the First and Second Rhode Island, and the Fourth and Eighth Connecticut. Action was soon to come.[3]

In the late summer of 1777, General William Howe sailed into Chesapeake Bay with a large British, Hessian, and Loyalist army. He marched into Pennsylvania, and defeated Washington at Brandywine and again at Germantown. On September 26, the American Capital of Philadelphia fell. Washington immediately called for reinforcements, and Varnum's Brigade was dispatched to Camden, New Jersey, to protect the river approaches to Philadelphia and stop the British from carrying supplies via the Delaware River. Varnum detached the Fourth and Eighth Connecticut to defend Fort Mifflin on Mud Island on the Pennsylvania side of the Delaware. The First and Second Rhode Island were sent to defend Fort Mercer, located at Red Bank on the New Jersey side of the Delaware.[4]

The attack came on October 22, when a force of twelve hundred Hessian Grenadiers, under the command of Colonel Carl von Donop, attempted to storm Fort Mercer. The Hessians approached to within forty yards of the fort, when the Rhode Islanders suddenly poured volley after volley into the Hessian ranks. Joseph Angell distinguished himself by poking his head above the works, and taking direct aim at the Hessians. When Captain Shaw fell, Angell took command of a section of the company and led it to a vulnerable section of the fort, where he continued to take aim at the Hessians for forty minutes, his comrades handing their muskets up to him to fire. The battle was short and decisive. The fort was not taken. The Hessians suffered over four hundred killed, wounded, and captured, including Colonel von Donop. Ten Rhode Islanders died, and twenty more were wounded, amongst them was Asa Potter of South Scituate who was killed on the parapet as a member of Captain Olney's Company. Potter was holding a salient, and was killed by members of his company as he was in the crossfire. For his actions during the battle, Joseph Angell was promoted to corporal. Lieutenant Thomas Hughes replaced Captain Shaw as the commander of his company.[5] After losing Fort Mifflin, and several indecisive actions around Philadelphia, the Continental Army retired to Valley Forge for the winter.

After entering Valley Forge, the Continentals would face their greatest challenge to date, not from Hessian muskets, or British bayonets, but from disease and privation. Sergeant Benjamin Boss was "reduced to wearing nothing but his shirt wrapped around, and tied on by what was left of the sleeves, and a pair of long wool stockings sent from home." After reviewing the Second Rhode Island, and seeing the condition Sergeant Boss was in, Washington said, "what a pity it is that such a fine young man should be reduced to such straights while fighting for his country." In March 1778, Sergeant Boss nearly died from putrid fever.[6] That winter the Second Rhode Island received new arms from France, and soon put them to use training with the Baron von Steuben in his new military maneuvers. Von Steuben selected the Second Rhode Island as his model regiment, by which he trained all others. By May of 1778, the tide of war had changed. France had entered the conflict, and the British were preparing to leave Philadelphia. Over the winter the First and Second Rhode Island Regiments had been consolidated, and the First was sent home to recruit African slaves and freemen, as well as Narragansett and Wampanoag Indians. On May 31, the Second Rhode Island received its first issue of clothing since leaving Rhode Island. On June 19, they

Sergeant Benjamin Boss: A recreation of Sergeant Boss might have appeared in the summer of 1778 during the Battles of Monmouth and Rhode Island. He wears a cocked hat, frock, long trousers, and Hessian shoes. He is armed with a captured British Short Land Pattern musket, and bayonet. He carries a captured British cartridge pouch, and canteen. He also carries a haversack to hold food, which was made at home, and a Scituate donation blanket. Photograph by author.

marched out of Valley Forge, newly equipped, and ready to fight the British as equals.[7]

After leaving Valley Forge, the Continentals found the rearguard of the British army near Monmouth, New Jersey, on June 27, 1778, and planned to attack the next morning. Varnum's Brigade would be in the front wave. The battle began as a division of Pennsylvanians attacked the British column, but were repulsed. Into the gap, Washington threw Varnum's Brigade. The battle lasted all day, with the Second Rhode Island fighting the British Guards in a small patch of forest near an open meadow. During the engagement General Varnum passed along the order to fix bayonets, and the brigade charged across the meadow and into the woodlot, routing the British Guards, the best troops in the King's Army. For the first time in the war, the Regulars had been routed by an American bayonet charge. For the Second Rhode Island, only ten men became casualties. Among them was Sergeant Benjamin Boss, who was wounded in the shoulder by a saber slash.[8] Monmouth was an American victory, and the first time the Continentals had succeeded in defeating the British in linear formations.

After Monmouth, the Second Rhode Island marched north to support another effort against the British in Newport. Varnum's Brigade was reorganized, and the First Rhode Island and Sherburne's Regiment, made up of men from Rhode Island and Connecticut, joined, while the Connecticut Regiments joined another brigade. Glover's Massachusetts Brigade, comprising the Marquis de Lafayette's Division, followed Varnum's Brigade. The Division marched through New Jersey, New York, and Connecticut, and Rhode Island, by the Plainfield Pike. On July 31, 1778 Varnum's Brigade arrived in Scituate, and camped near the Angell Tavern. Sergeant Major Jeremiah Greenman of the Second Rhode Island described the encampment in his journal:

> F 31. this morn started from Vallington (Vollington, CT)/ proceeded on our rout as far as Coentry about 18 milds from providance ware we grounded our arms/ it began to wrain/ we took up our arms and put them in a shed/ about 4 o Clock we peraded marcht 6 milds to Scituate to angells tavern ware we pitched our tents & was order'd to wash all our Cloath & clean our arms.

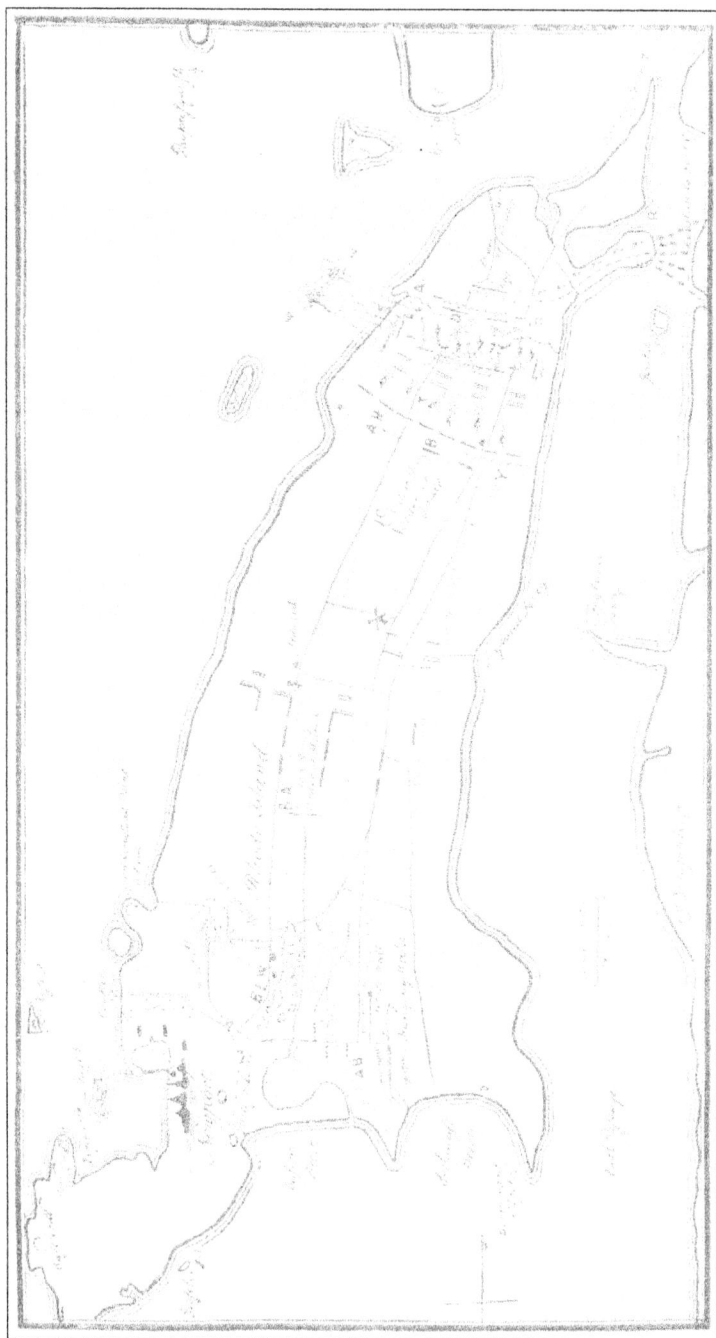

General Sullivan's official map of the Rhode Island Campaign.
Rhode Island State Archives.

August, 1778 on a March S 1. Continuing in Scituate washing our cloaths/ two Rij't joyn'd us Colo Shurburns & Colo Webbs & sum arttillira/ we hear that the French fleet is alround Newport, & took sum frigates/ was order'd to hold our Selves in readiness to march in the morning-[9]

From Scituate, the Second Rhode Island marched to Providence, and then to Rhode Island where they would fight the Battle of Rhode Island on August 29, 1778. Here the Second would again show merit. With the support of Sherburne's Regiment, they prevented the First Rhode Island from being overrun by the Hessians. Only four men were wounded. The battle was a draw.[10]

After the Battle of Rhode Island, the Second Rhode Island was sent to guard North Kingston. While here the men were involved in constant mutinies and desertion attempts. Colonel Angell quickly stepped in, and floggings were held daily to dissuade the men from committing violent acts. Amongst them was Caleb Eddy of western Scituate. Eddy was a private in Captain Stephen Olney's Company. He was accused of stealing the pocket book of a fellow solider; Eddy was placed under arrest, and faced a court martial. Rather then face the punishment, Eddy deserted, and escaped into the forest of Scituate. While the Second Rhode Island was at home, recruiting parties were dispatched throughout the state looking for men. Only forty were enlisted; of these, three came from Scituate.[11] In November of 1779, after the British had evacuated Newport, the Second Rhode Island was reassigned to the Main Army under Washington, then in winter camp at Morristown, New Jersey. For many a Rhode Islander, this would be their final winter.[12]

The death of the Second Rhode Island Regiment occurred on June 23, 1780 at Springfield, New Jersey. The Second Rhode Island, and a Hope Furnace cannon was assigned to guard a bridge over the Rahway River. With only 160 officers and men in line, the Second Rhode Island held for forty minutes, protecting the bridge from the British Grenadiers. The British managed to flank the Second Rhode Island through an apple orchard, but were repulsed.[13] When the smoke cleared, only 120 Rhode Islanders were still standing. Among the wounded was Sergeant Benjamin Boss, whose left ear was shot away. Corporal Joseph Angell was also wounded by a cannon shot while taking cover in the orchard. After the stand on the Rahway Bridge, the Second was no longer considered an effective fighting regiment, and with low strength in both the First Rhode Island and Sherburne's Regiment, the three were to be consolidated into the Rhode Island Regiment.[14]

In January 1781, the consolidation was complete, and with only one Rhode Island Regiment, command was given to Colonel Christopher Greene. Colonel Israel Angell was forced into retirement. In May, Colonel Greene was killed by Tory raiders, and was replaced by Lieutenant Colonel Jeremiah Olney. The Rhode Island Regiment then marched to Yorktown, Virginia. On the night of October 14, 1781, the Light Infantry Company, led by Captain Stephen Olney, was the first over the works at the capture of Redoubt Number Ten.[15] Victory was soon achieved.

During eight years of war with the Continental Army, Rhode Islanders had been at all of the battles, save Brandywine, Germantown, and Saratoga. Despite constant hardships, such as ragged clothing, little food, and no pay, the Rhode Island Continentals had fought well, and had never run. Over one hundred Scituate men served in the Continental Army; at over ten men died. The Continentals, who suffered some of the greatest hardships ever known to man, and persevered, won an incredible victory, despite the odds against them.

CHAPTER ELEVEN

The Rhode Island Campaign

A fter the signing of the Franco-American Alliance in 1778, France made plans to send a large naval and land force to America. Washington decided that Newport should be retaken, and directed the French force there. Washington detached one of his ablest generals, John Sullivan of New Hampshire, to take command. It seemed as though Newport would finally be liberated.

One of General Sullivan's first acts was to call out six thousand Massachusetts and Rhode Island militia to serve for three months. Scituate voted to tax itself £77 to "provide 1,246.5 pounds of bread, 794.75 pounds of pork, and 154 pounds of beef for the men upon the campaign." Also collected by donation were many axes. For the campaign against Rhode Island, Scituate stripped its arsenal of weapons to provide them for the militia, this included the remaining stock at the Angell Tavern. In addition, all firearms in the town that belonged to men upon the Alarm List, and those excused from service due to medical disabilities were requisitioned. For this their owners were given promissory notes ranging in price of £3-10 depending upon the condition of the firearm. These notes could be cashed in, however, if the musket was not returned. Despite these provisions, nearly a third of the Scituate men would see combat without a weapon. Scituate received the call on July 15, 1778, when General Sullivan sent the following message to Major Joseph Knight, as the British were again threatening Providence after having attacked Bristol:

> Pray, delay no time, for by the delay of one hour we may lose the town of Providence; let each man take three days provision, and wait there for further orders.[1]

From Providence, Major Knight marched the Third Providence County Regiment to Tiverton, where they joined West's Brigade.

For the campaign against Rhode Island, the Third Providence County Regiment was again reorganized. Captain Jonathan Knight became a member of his brother's staff, while Captain Stephen Kimball remained in Scituate to command a small battalion of invalids and those not capable of making the campaign. Captain John Potter, who had been promoted from the Third Company, now led the First Company. Low in strength, the Scituate Hunters were disbanded, and an Eighth Company was added to the Regiment, commanded by Captain Nathan Ralfe, formerly Lieutenant in the Fifth Company. With Lieutenant Colonel John Colwell on duty in Providence, command fell to Major Knight. He would be commanding eight battalion companies; they were numbered and commanded by:

First Company:
    Captain John Potter, 75 officers and men.
Second Company:
    Captain George Dorrance, 67 officers and men
Third Company:
    Captain Coman Smith, 123 officers and men
Fourth Company:
    Captain Isaac Paine, 109 officers and men
Fifth Company:
    Captain Samuel Wilbur, 76 officers and men
Sixth Company:
    Captain William Howard, 64 officers and men
Seventh Company:
    Captain Jonathan Medbury, 32 officers and men
Eighth Company:
    Captain Nathan Ralfe, 67 officers and men
Total: 613 officers and men.

Unlike many other militia regiments, the Third Providence County Regiment was well led, organized, and disciplined. The regiment contained eight full-strength companies, unlike most other regiments, which only had at most three hundred men. Also, it contained a regimental staff, comprising an adjutant, clerk, quartermaster, sergeant major, and surgeon. Furthermore, it was led by qualified field and company officers. This would have a great impact on events to come.

Upon arrival in Tiverton in late July 1778, the Third Providence County Regiment joined the 412 officers and men in Colonel Chad Brown's Second Providence County Regiment. The two regiments formed West's Brigade, numbering 1025 men.[2] The Brigade spent several weeks in Tiverton, drilling and receiving supplies for the campaign. Reinforcements arrived daily, and soon Lafayette's Division of Continentals arrived. Attached to Lafayette's Division was Brigadier General Ezekiel Cornell's Brigade of Rhode Island State troops. On the night of August 9, with the French planning to support the campaign, the American army began landing upon Rhode Island. General Sullivan arranged the army in three lines. His best men, the two Continental brigades under Glover and Varnum, as well as Cornell's Rhode Island State Brigade, formed the first line under the Marquis de Lafayette. The second line consisted of four brigades of Massachusetts and Rhode Island Militia under Major General Nathanael Greene. The third line, or the Reserves, was composed of West's Brigade. In total the Americans had nearly ten thousand men in the field, compared to seven thousand British in Newport. The campaign looked as though it would succeed, but soon found itself falling apart.[3]

On August 15, the American forces began their siege of Newport. Amongst the cannon used were twenty-four-pound cannon made at the Hope Furnace. West's Brigade was assigned to guard the baggage and the rear. On August 20, the plan fell apart, as the French fleet sailed to Boston to repair, after being grounded by a large hurricane. Washington soon wrote to Sullivan that ten thousand Regulars were sailing immediately to Newport as reinforcements. The situation was critical. Sullivan turned to his brigade and division commanders and asked them what to do: attack or retreat? Amongst those who responded was Brigadier General West, who suggested continuing the siege, but leaving open a line of retreat. In response to attack, West wrote, "However if upon the whole your Excellency thinks the sooner the most advisable to storm their Lines I think the sooner the better; and be assured that no one shall be more ready cheerfully to obey your Excellencys Commands than his Most Obedient Servant." The men of Scituate were ready for action.[4]

Battle of Rhode Island
August 29 - 31, 1778

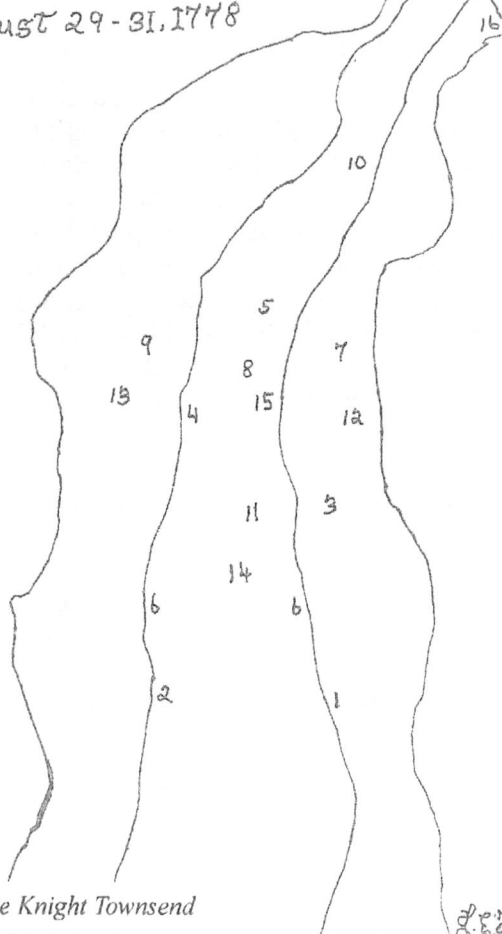

16
10
5
9
8   7
13 4 15 12
11   3
14
6   6
2   1

Map by Joyce Knight Townsend

1. East Main Road
2. West Main Road
3. Quaker Hill
4. Turkey Hill
5. Butt's Hill
6. American Light Infantry
   ambush Crown Forces
7. Glover's Brigade
8. Cornell's Brigade
9. Varnum's Brigade

10. West's Brigade
11. Crown Forces deploy for battle
12. Regulars attack Cornell and
    Glover
13. Hessians attack Varnum
14. Crown Forces retire
15. West's Brigade deploys
16. Americans retreat across the
    Sakonnet River

On the night of August 28, 1778, Sullivan abandoned his siege lines and retired to the north end of Rhode Island. By morning the Americans were entrenched upon the high ground in Portsmouth, still maintaining their battle lines. West's Brigade was placed a half-mile from the first line, in a reserve position near Founder's Brook. After his line was in place, Sullivan dispatched the Marquis de Lafayette to Boston to persuade the French to return.[5] On the morning of August 29, Lieutenant General Robert Pigot, the British commander, sent half his army out of Newport in an attempt to capture the American forces.

The Battle of Rhode Island started at 7:00 a.m. when two battalions of American light infantry valiantly attempted to hold off the British and Hessian soldiers on the two main roads running the length of the island. The Crown Forces suffered heavy casualties, and when reinforcements were brought up, the Americans retreated to the main line. On the East Main Road, the Regulars in the 22nd, 38th, 43rd, and 54th Regiments of Foot constantly attacked Glover's and Cornell's Brigades, and were repulsed at every advance. On the left, Varnum's Rhode Island Brigade repulsed three separate Hessian attacks. West's Brigade was never called into action, but felt the effects of long-range artillery fire. By 3:00 the battle had ended; American casualties were 211; the Crown Forces, 260.[6]

The Marquis de Lafayette arrived on the night of the twenty-ninth, and reported to Sullivan that the French would not return. The situation was now dire; General Sullivan had to retreat, or General Clinton and his reinforcements would capture the remainder of the American Army. The two lines remained in place during August 30 as a ceasefire was declared, and both sides buried their dead and tended to the wounded, the Americans taking theirs off the island. In a clever ruse, Sullivan kept his tents pitched and his forward sentries occupied, while he ferried his artillery and heavy baggage to the crossing. General Sullivan then called upon Brigadier General John Glover of Massachusetts. Glover had saved the Continental Army in New York, and had rowed Washington across the Delaware to attack Trenton in December 1776. His brigade contained a large number of New England fisherman and sailors. Their task would be to use the large number of small boats that General Sullivan had commandeered to ferry the army across the Sackonnet River, via Howland's Ferry. Sullivan assigned Lafayette to cover the retreat; West's Brigade was called upon to serve as the rearguard. The brigade came onto line and deployed into a large skirmish line three hundred yards from the Crown Forces encamped on Quaker and Turkey Hills. That night, the British pickets of the 22nd Regiment of Foot advanced close to the line, and several men of West's Brigade were killed and wounded. Amongst them was Sergeant Levi Lee of the Second Providence County Regiment who exclaimed, "The damned eternal souls shoot pretty close. Don't mind, my boys stick to 'em." In the early morning hours of August 31, 1778, with all of the American forces off of Rhode Island, West's Brigade was pulled off the line and was the last to cross back to Tiverton. Lafayette would later claim, "Not a man was left behind." The Third Providence County Regiment had been successful in covering the retreat, losing only a few men in a very critical position. The Rhode Island Campaign was over.[7]

After spending several days at Tiverton, West's Brigade was promptly dismissed, and the men returned to their homes. Captain Isaac Paine and some men from his company volunteered to stay behind to help train the militia. For their actions during the campaign, Major Joseph Knight was promoted to lieutenant colonel, and Captain Stephen Kimball was promoted to major. Lieutenant Colonel John Colwell was promoted to Colonel, while Lieutenant Colonel Knight retained control of the battalion. In Lieutenant Colonel Knight's report of the campaign, he lists in his return of the First, Third, and Fifth Companies, "272 privates, with 101 firelocks, 26 bayonets, and 43 cartouches (cartridge boxes)." In November 1778, the Rhode Island General Assembly granted the men of the Third Providence County Regiment £3,021.15 in bounty money for their participation in the campaign.[8] The Rhode Island Campaign had been a success though Newport was not taken, the Franco-American Alliance had been tested, and for the second time, the Scituate Militia had shown its merit in battle

A woodcut of the hilt of a sword presented to the Marquis de Lafayette by Congress for his role in the retreat from Rhode Island on August 30-31, 1778. Stone, *Allies.*

CHAPTER TWELVE

The Arrival of the French

F ollowing the Battle of Rhode Island, French forces were slow to return to America. In 1779, with Crown Forces spread very thin, it was decided to remove the British garrison from Newport and send them to New York. In the summer of 1779, the Marquis de Lafayette was dispatched to France to persuade the French to send troops to support the Americans. Following the evacuation of Newport, a new French fleet as well as a division of French Regulars under the Comte de Rochambeau was dispatched to America.[1]

On July 11, 1780 after seventy days at sea, the French arrived in Newport. A large British force was dispatched from New York to attack them. On July 27, 1780, Lieutenant Colonel Joseph Knight received the following message from the Governor, via Rufus Hopkins:

> By express from the Governor I am requested to direct you forthwith to muster together the regiment under your command, completely equipped with arms and ammunition and six days provision; you are therefore hereby directed accordingly, and rendezvous at Providence as soon as possible, where you are to be ready to receive further orders, the reason is said to be in consequence of Gen. Clinton's coming from New York with eight or ten thousand troops to attack the French army and fleet at Newport.[2]

Lieutenant Colonel Knight marched to Providence, where he waited for several days, and then returned to Scituate. The British turned back, and the French were safe.

The French remained in Newport for a year, training and filling their ranks. Finally on the morning of June 10, 1781, the French troops left Newport and marched down the Plainfield Pike to

A woodcut of the Angell Tavern, based on Beaman's description.
Bennet and Lenihan.

reinforce the Continentals. On June 19, they arrived in Scituate. For four days the French encamped at the Angell Tavern, waiting while their baggage and cannon caught up. First to arrive was the Royal Deux Ponts Regiment, followed by the Soisonnais, Saintonge, and Bourbonnais Regiments. Accompanying each regiment was a battery of artillery. Several Scituate civilians were hired by the French to conduct their artillery down the Plainfield Pike by the use of their oxen. The French regiments each spent one day at the encampment and then moved on, as to not overburden the surrounding area with their needs. In Scituate Rochambeau met up with his cavalry, under the Duke de Luzon, who had been holding his left flank at Lebanon, Connecticut. The Third Providence County Regiment escorted the French, while many of the French officers stayed in personnel residences along the Pike.[3]

Many legends abound in Scituate about the French. One of them is that the Marquis de Lafayette had an ill stomach and could not eat, so Mrs. Angell made him some porridge "that set his stomach just right." Another legend is that a French biscuit cart turned over on a hill, and the people of Scituate were allowed to collect the biscuits. Today the area is known as Biscuit Hill.[4] A French soldier of the Bourbonnais Regiment died at the Angell Tavern, and his remains were buried in the Battey Meeting House Cemetery. The French soldiers also held concerts each night, and people came from as far as Pomfret, Connecticut, to hear them.[5] After four days, the French marched on to join the Continental Army at Peekskill, New York. Scituate would always remember the French, and after the war several French soldiers returned to Scituate to marry the women they had met there.

Throughout the summer of 1781, the Light Infantry Division of the Continental Army chased Cornwallis throughout Virginia. In the division was a company of Rhode Islanders under Captain Stephen Olney, with him were four Scituate soldiers. From Peekskill the French marched to Virginia, where Lieutenant General Charles Cornwallis was besieged on the Yorktown peninsula. The Franco-American force moved into position and conducted a siege operation against the entrenched Crown Army. After a siege of twenty-one days, the British surrendered on

October 19, 1781, and marched out of their entrenchments to stack their arms, and colors.[6]

After two more years of indecisive action, Charlestown, South Carolina, was evacuated; and after the signing of the definitive peace treaty, New York was finally evacuated on November 25, 1783. It had been nearly ten years since the war began. The people of Scituate rejoiced in the end of the war. Freedom had been won, but at a terrible cost.

CHAPTER THIRTEEN

Aftermath

S cituate was forever changed by the Revolution. In 1774, the
population was 3,601. In 1781, it was 1,635. In 1781, Scituate
was divided in two, and the western half of the town was named
Foster. After the war was over, many of the younger men of both
Scituate and Foster packed up what few possessions they had, and
moved to the frontier of New York and Ohio. The Revolution had
been costly for Scituate: over seven hundred men had served,
more than fifty were dead, and the town was £50,000 in debt.[1]

The Scituate Militia continued to serve, now drilling only four
times per year. The Second, Fourth, and Sixth Companies were
detached, and became the Foster Militia, and were designated as
the Sixth Providence County Regiment. In 1787 Lieutenant
Colonel Joseph Knight was promoted to colonel of the Third
Providence County Regiment, now reduced to only four
companies. During the War of 1812, the Regiment would serve
guarding the Kingston shore, while never being engaged in
combat.[2] In 1841, the Angell Tavern, where so much history had
taken place during the Revolution, burnt down. In 1842, the
Scituate Militia was again called into action, and fought at the
Battle of Acoates Hill, a bloodless skirmish during the Rhode
Island political fiasco known as the Dorr Rebellion. In 1852, the
Third Providence County Regiment was disbanded, ending over
one hundred years of service. From Crown Point, to the Battle of
Rhode Island, to the Dorr Rebellion, the men of Scituate had been
in the thick of it all.

Scituate remained a small town, and became a large textile
manufacturing center in the 1850s. In 1861, the men of Scituate
again answered the call to serve in the Civil War. Over four
hundred left; fifty-five never came home. In 1914, Scituate would
again change forever, as the Rhode Island General Assembly,

invoking the power of eminent domain, condemned over 16,000 acres of land to provide a reservoir for drinking water for the people of the state. In effect, Scituate was nearly wiped off the map. The villages of Ashland, Kent, Richmond, Rockland, South Scituate, and Wilbur Hollow were soon under a hundred feet of water.[3]

The people of these villages suffered greatly. Many burned their property, and some committed suicide rather than turn their land in. Many were forced to sell homesteads that their families had lived in for nearly two centuries. Most disturbing for them was leaving behind their dead, buried in small burial plots throughout the reservoir area. Amongst those who suffered the most were the Knights. At this time the family owned most of Kent, Richmond, and South Scituate. Despite trying to save the homes and lands they had lived upon for over two hundred years, they had to leave. Many simply left their homes and businesses as they were, and removed to western Massachusetts, or settled in other areas of Rhode Island. One elderly Knight woman even attempted to hold the reservoir men back with a family shotgun. The Knights, however, were lucky in one respect. Because their graveyards were out of the flood plain, the buried were allowed to stay where they were; rather than being removed to a new cemetery in Rockland. Amongst those allowed to remain was Colonel Joseph Knight. To this day, the Scituate Reservoir is remembered by the Knights, and still brings with it sadness, as they remember what their family had to give up. In time the reservoir became part of Scituate, and the people moved on with their lives. To this day, the town of Scituate has not taken one drop from the reservoir.[4]

Still today sections of Scituate untouched by the reservoir have the look of the eighteenth century. A small monument marked, "In Memory of Scituate's Revolutionary Patriots" stands on the Town Green. In the village of Clayville, one can still walk the path followed by the American and French soldiers on their way to the war. Many homes of the men who fought in the Revolution still stand. The sole surviving Hope Furnace cannon is displayed in front of the Hope Library.

In backyards and in the forest stand small slate and granite stones, mute testaments to a soldier's grave. Most are only carved with the man's initials, or a name and simple epitaph. One such

Memorial: This simple bronze plaque is dedicated to Scituate's Revolutionary soldiers. Photograph by author.

tribute is to Jonathan Briggs of Hope. In 1777 he was twenty-two years old, and enlisted to serve for the duration of the war as a private in Captain William Tew's Company of Colonel Israel Angell's Second Rhode Island Regiment. Briggs served for six years, and fought at Red Bank, Monmouth, and Yorktown. When he died in 1837, his small marble memorial was carved with a simple passage to mark his final resting place as that of a patriot.

> When tyranny was blazing brand
> And hostile armies cleared our land
> This brave young farmer pledged his life
> Till Yorktown closed the bloody strife.

On the 19th of April each year the long roll again echoes through the woods of Scituate as the men again answer the call to freedom. The men and women of Scituate, whom contributed so much of themselves and their lives to win freedom, are not forgotten.

EPILOGUE

Corporal Joseph Angell returned to South Scituate and became a
farmer. He married and raised two sons. He died in 1808.[1]

Sergeant Benjamin Boss returned to his farm nearly nine years
after leaving. He continued to farm, and became a captain
during the War of 1812, performing coastwatching duty at
North Kingstown. In 1846, after seeing several of his
grandsons off to fight in Mexico, he is quoted to have said, "If I
was but a young man, I'd be there." He died in 1848.[2]

Private William Boswell enlisted in the Second Rhode Island
Regiment and fought throughout the Revolution. He also
became an American citizen. He purchased a farm in Foster
and raised a large family. Today his grave in western Foster is
marked by a small military headstone and the flag of the
country he came so far to fight for.[3]

Colonel John Colwell moved to Foster and resumed farming.[4]

Brigadier General Ezekiel Cornell became a member of the United
States Congress, and after serving three terms returned to
Scituate. After failing to establish himself as a merchant, he
moved to Milford, Massachusetts, where he died in 1800.[5]

Dr. Caleb Fisk returned to Scituate, and founded the village of
Fiskeville. He later became president of the Rhode Island
Medical Society, and continued to acquire land and money. He
died in 1832.[6]

Captain Joseph Kimball became a farmer, and was a member of
the Scituate Town Council. He died in 1803.[7]

Major Stephen Kimball became Collector of Taxes in Scituate. He
died in 1805.[8]

Colonel Joseph Knight returned to his farm and continued to
acquire land. In 1803 he opened up a tavern on the Plainfield

Pike, and later was elected to the Scituate Town Council and became president. He retired from the militia in 1800, and remained on his Tunk Hill farm. His wife Elizabeth, who had tended the farm while he was at war, died in 1823. Colonel Joseph Knight, a distinguished soldier, politician, farmer, and father died on February 27, 1825. He was buried in a corner of his farm. A small slate stone engraved with his name and date of death is all that marks his grave. Colonel Knight produced a long line of soldiers who fought in every major conflict this country has ever engaged in. Twelve of his grandsons would fight in the Civil War; two would not come home. In 1913, Scituate erected a monument to her Civil War dead. During the dedication speech, Colonel Knight was described as"Scituate's bravest son."[9]

Captain Jonathan Knight, Jr. continued to operate his brother's sawmill, and became part of the Scituate Town Council. He died in 1818. Today the forests of Scituate have surrounded his grave.[10]

Lieutenant Colonel Jeremiah Olney, became a merchant in Providence. He later became a member of the Rhode Island General Assembly, and died in 1812.[11]

Captain Isaac Paine became a member of the Foster Town Council. Today the elementary school in Foster is named after him.[12]

Brigadier General William West returned to his "Great House," and became Town Moderator. He fell into hard times after the war and was forced to sell off all of his land. When he died in 1816, he could not even afford a headstone.[13]

Captain Samuel Wilbur became a farmer, and purchased a 124-acre apple farm and cider mill in Rockland. He fell into ill health and died in 1795, $150 in debt.[14]

APPENDIX

Scituate men who served in the militia and Continental Line during the Revolution.

The following is a list of Scituate men who served during the Revolution. This list is garnered from Beaman's *Historical Sketch,* Field's *Defenses*, Anthony Walker's *So Few the Brave*, the Town Records of Foster and Scituate, and papers in the author's collection. Over seven hundred Scituate men served, but due to the ravages of time, these are all that are known today. For the sake of brevity, the following abbreviations are used to describe rank. (Corporal: Corp. Sergeant: Sgt. Ensign: Ens. Lieutenant: Lt. Captain: Capt. Major: Maj. Lieutenant Colonel: Lt. Col. Colonel: Col. Brigadier General: Brig. Gen.) The highest rank achieved during the war is used. If no rank is given, it is assumed that the man served as a private. When a designation such as "1st Co." appears next to a name, this man served in the given company in the Third Providence County Regiment. The abbreviation "Hughes' Co. 2nd R.I. Regt" means that the man served in the given captain's company in the Second Rhode Island Regiment of the Continental Line. The companies of Captains Stephen Kimball and Jeremiah Olney were in the Second Rhode Island Regiment of 1775-1777. Neither man commanded a company in the three-year Second Rhode Island Regiment of 1777. "R.I. Regt of 1781" infers to the regiment created from the consolidation of the First and Second Rhode Island, as well as Sherburne's Additional Regiment in 1781. If no regiment information is given, it is unavailable. Name spelling remains the same as it appears upon the muster rolls.

Aldrich, Abel. J. Olney's Co. 2nd R.I. Regt. C. Olney's Co. 2nd R.I. Regt.
Aldrich, Abraham. Scituate Hunters.
Aldrich, James.
Aldrich, Joel. Lt. 2nd Co.
Aldrich, Noah. 3rd Co.

Aldrich, Samuel. Ens. 2nd Co.
Allen, Brian. 5th Co.
Allen, Joseph.
Allen, Josiah.
Almy, Jeremiah. 1st Co.
Andrews, James.
Andrews, Jeremiah.
Angell, Abel. 5th Co.
Angell, Abraham. Kimball's Co. 2nd R.I. Regt.
Angell, Andrew. Capt. Alarm List.
Angell, Daniel. 1st Co.
Angell, Jabel. Lt. 3rd Co.
Angell, Jesse.
Angell, Job. Capt. Alarm List.
Angell, Joseph. Shaw's Co. 2nd R.I. Regt. Corp. S. Olney's
     Co. 2nd R.I. Regt. Varnum's Brigade Guard.
Angell, Joseph. 6th Co. J. Olney's Co. 2nd R.I. Regt.
Angell, Joshua.
Angell, Nehemiah. Scituate Hunters. Ens. Kimball's Co. 2nd
     R.I. Regt.
Angell, Pardon.
Angell, Samuel. Ens. 3rd Co.
Anthony, John. Surgeon's Mate. 3rd Providence County Regt.
Arnold, Benjamin. Kimball's Co. 2nd R.I. Regt. Ens. Dexter's
     Co. 2nd R.I. Regt. Arrested December 1777. Cashiered and
     dismissed January 1778.
Arnold, Edward. Drummer. S. Olney's Co. 2nd R.I. Regt.
Arnold, Jabez. Kimball's Co. 2nd R.I. Regt.
Arnold, Oliver. 2nd Co. and 6th Co.
Arnold, Othniel. Scituate Hunters. Corp. Kimball's Co. 2nd
     R.I. Regt.
Arnold, Thomas.
Arnold, William. Corp. Kimball's Co. 2nd R.I. Regt.
Arwin, William. Quartermaster. 3rd Providence County Regt.
Aston Jr., Gideon. Corp. 5th Co.
Aston Sr., Gideon. Corp. 5th Co.
Aston, Isaiah. 1st Co.
Aston, Thomas. 5th Co.
Atwood, John. Sgt. Scituate Hunters.

Austin, Isaiah. 1st Co.
Austin, Paskow. J. Olney's Co. 2nd R.I. Regt.
Bacon, Benjain. 1st Co.
Baker, Daniel. Ens. Alarm List.
Baker, John. Ens. Alarm List.
Baker, Jeremiah. 5th Co.
Barden, Jonathan. 4th Co.
Barden, Matthew. R.I. Regt of 1781.
Barns, William. 5th Co.
Basset, John. 3rd Co.
Basset, Zachariah. Kimball's Co. 2nd R.I. Regt.
Bates, Nathan. Ens. 1st Co.
Battey, John. 5th Co.
Battey, William. 5th Co.
Bennet Jr., John. 1st Co.
Bennet Jr., Joseph. 5th Co.
Bennet Sr., Joseph. 5th Co.
Bennet, Loney. 5th Co.
Bennett, Asher. 4th Co.
Bennett, Benjamin. Dexter's Co. 2nd R.I. Regt. R.I. Regt. of 1781.
Bennett, Edward. 1st Co. J. Olney's Co. 2nd R.I. Regt.
Bennett, Joseph. 1st Co. J. Olney's Co. 2nd R.I. Regt.
Bennett, Micajah. R.I. Regt. of 1781.
Bickford, Thomas. Kimball's Co. 2nd R.I. Regt.
Biddleford, William. 5th Co.
Bishop, Ezekiel.
Bishop, Naman. Corp. J. Olney's Co. 2nd R.I. Regt.
Bishop, Oliver. J. Olney's Co. 2nd R.I. Regt.
Blackman, John. Clerk. 3rd Providence County Regt.
Blackmar, Amaziah. Kimball's Co. 2nd R.I. Regt.
Blanchard, John. Tew's Co. 2nd R.I. Regt. R.I. Regt. of 1781
Blanchard, Isaac. Ens. 2nd Co.
Blancher, James. Kimball's Co. 2nd R.I. Regt.
Booth, John. J. Olney's Co. 2nd R.I. Regt.
Boss, Benjamin. Kimball's Co. 2nd R.I. Regt. Sgt. Hughes' Co. 2nd R.I. Regt. Sgt. R.I. Regt. of 1781.
Boswell, William. Tew's Co. 2nd R.I. Regt. R.I. Regt. of 1781.
Bosworth, Benajah. 1st Co.

Bosworth, Joseph. Kimball's Co. 2nd R.I. Regt. S. Olney's Co.
  2nd R.I. Regt. Died May 21, 1778 at Valley Forge.
Bowen, Abial. Adjutant. West's Brigade.
Brayton, Freeborn. 7th Co.
Brayton, John. 7th Co.
Brayton, Thomas. 2nd Co.
Bridges, Obadiah. J. Olney's Co. 2nd R.I. Regt.
Brigford, Thomas. Drummer. Scituate Hunters.
Briggs, Abraham. Corp. 5th Co.
Briggs, Allen. J. Olney's Co. 2nd R.I. Regt.
Briggs, Job. 5th Co.
Briggs, Jonathan. Tew's Co. 2nd R.I. Regt.
Briggs, Joseph. 1st Co. J. Olney's Co. 2nd R.I. Regt.
Briggs, Robert. 4th Co.
Brock, Ebenezer.
Brock, Ezekiel. 5th Co.
Brown, Charles. Kimball's Co. 2nd R.I. Regt.
Brown, Jesse. 3rd Co.
Brown, Phillip. 1st, 5th, and 6th Co.
Brown, Samuel.
Brownell, William. Scituate Hunters. Sgt. 1st Co. Lt. 3rd Co.
Bucklen, Squire. Kimball's Co. 2nd R.I. Regt. Lt. 4th Co.
Burgess, William. 2nd Co.
Burlingame, Abner. Scituate Hunters.
Burlingame, David.
Burlingame, Jeremiah. Corp. J. Olney's Co. 2nd R.I. Regt.
Burlingame, John. R.I. Regt. of 1781.
Burlingame, Nehemiah. Lt. 7th Co.
Burlingame, Pardon. Ens. 7th Co.
Burlingame, Solomon. Kimball's Co. 2nd R.I. Regt.
Cappel, Peter. J. Olney's Co. 2nd R.I. Regt.
Carpenter, Joseph. Lt. Alarm List.
Carver, Oliver. Scituate Hunters.
Carver, Joseph. 6th Co.
Chapman, Rufus. Kimball's Co. 2nd R.I. Regt. S. Olney's Co.
  2nd R.I. Regt.
Cheney, Nathaniel. 6th Co.
Chilton, Ezra.
Churchill, James. Heath's Co. Sergeant's Massachusetts Regt.

Clark, Eleazer. J. Olney's Co. 2nd R.I. Regt.
Cocran, Moses. Kimball's Co. 2nd R.I. Regt. Corp. Thayer's
  Co. Quebec Expedition. Died in Maine, 1775.
Cole, James. 4th Co.
Cole Jr., John. Lt. 4th Co.
Cole Jr., Richard. Ens. 4th Co.
Cole, Jesse. 3rd Co.
Colgrove, Caleb. Kimball's Co. 2nd R.I. Regt.
Collins, Abel. 5th Co.
Collins, Christopher. 1st Co. J. Olney's Co. 2nd R.I. Regt.
Collins, Joseph. 1st Co.
Colvin, Benjamin. 5th Co.
Colvin, Benoni.
Colvin, Joseph. C. Olney's Co. 2nd R.I. Regt.
Colvin, Jr. Thomas. J. Olney's Co. 2nd R.I. Regt.
Colvin, Moses. 1st Co.
Colvin, Noah. 5th Co.
Colvin, Peleg. 5th Co.
Colvin, Rufus. 5th Co.
Colwell, John. Col. 3rd Providence County Regt.
Coman, Zephaniah. Kimball's Co. 2nd R.I. Regt.
Cornell, Ezekiel. Lt. Col. 3rd Providence County Regt. and 2nd
  R.I. Regt. Brig. Gen. R.I. State Brigade.
Cornell, Gideon. Lt. Scituate Hunters.
Cornell, Nathaniel. Scituate Hunters.
Crossman, Ashael. 2nd Co.
Curtis, Bethuel. Kimball's Co. 2nd R.I. Regt.
Dailey, Solomon. J. Olney's Co. 2nd R.I. Regt.
Davis, Jeremiah. Capt. 4th Co.
Davis, Joseph. Lt. 3rd Co.
Davis, Joseph. 6th Co.
Davis, Simon. 6th Co.
Daw, Edward. J. Olney's Co. 2nd R.I. Regt.
Dexter, Daniel. 1st Co.
Dexter, William. R.I. Regt. of 1781.
Dobee, Jonathan. Kimball's Co. 2nd R.I. Regt.
  Corp. Hughes' Co. 2nd R.I. Regt.
Dorrance, George. Capt. 2nd Co.
Eddy, Caleb. S. Olney's Co. 2nd R.I. Regt.

Eddy, Jarvis.

Eddy, John. 4th Co.

Eddy, Thomas. Scituate Hunters.

Eddy, William. Scituate Hunters.

Edmonds, William. Kimball's Co. 2nd R.I. Regt. Hughes' Co.
2nd R.I. Regt.

Edmunds, Eliphalett. R.I. Regt. of 1781.

Edwards Jr., John. 1st Co. Died at Warwick, 1776.

Edwards, Christopher. 1st Co.

Edwards, Ephraim. 5th Co.

Edwards, Nicholas.

Edwards, Stephen. 1st Co. J. Olney's Co. 2nd R.I. Regt.

Edwards, William. J. Olney's Co. 2nd R.I. Regt. Hughes' Co.
2nd R.I. Regt.

Eldridge, Samuel. 1st Co. J. Olney's Co. 2nd R.I. Regt.

Eldridge, William.

Ewell, John. 2nd R.I. Regt.

Fairbanks, William. 5th Co.

Field, Nehemiah. Ens. J. Olney's Co. 2nd R.I. Regt.

Field, Thomas. Lt. 5th Co.

Field, William. Capt. 7th Co.

Fisk Jr., Job. Lt. Scituate Artillery Company.

Fisk, Aaron. Corp. 1st Co. Potter's Co. 2nd R.I. Regt. Killed in
Action June 28, 1778. Monmouth, New Jersey.

Fisk, Caleb. Surgeon. 1st Co. and 3rd Providence County Regt.

Fisk, Daniel. 1st Co.

Fisk, Elihue.

Fisk, Hezekiah. 6th Co.

Fisk, Job. 6th Co. Scituate Hunters.

Fisk, Moses. 5th Co.

Fisk, Noah. 5th Co.

Fisk, Oliver. 1st Co. Died as a prisoner of war onboard the
Good Intent in New York, May 30, 1778.

Fisk, William. 5th Co.

Foster, William. Hughes' Co. 2nd R.I. Regt. Died January 23,
1778 at Valley Forge.

Franklin Jr., Uriah. 1st Co.

Franklin, David. Sgt. 5th Co.

Franklin, Edward.

Franklin, John.
Franklin, Joseph.
Franklin, Nathan. 1st Co.
Fuller, Francis.
Fuller Jr., Francis. 1st Co.
Fuller, John. J. Olney's Co. 2nd R.I. Regt.
Gile, John. 5th Co.
Goodspeed, Simeon. R.I. Regt. of 1781.
Gordon, George. R.I. Regt. of 1781.
Gorton, Benjamin. 5th Co. J. Olney's Co. 2nd R.I. Regt.
Grant, Jr. John. J. Olney's Co. 2nd R.I. Regt.
Graves, Constant. 1st Co.
Graves, John. 1st Co.
Gray, Benjamin. R.I. Regt. of 1781.
Greene, George. R.I. Regt. of 1781.
Griffiths, Paul. 4th Co.
Griffiths, Southward. 4th Co.
Gunnison, John. 1st Co.
Hall, Benjamin. 6th Co.
Hall, Joseph. R.I. Regt. of 1781.
Hammond, Amos. 2nd Co.
Hammond, John. Ens. 2nd Co.
Handy, Ebenezer. 1st Co.
Harpers, John. 3rd Co.
Harris, Andrew. 3rd Co.
Harris, Ashael. 3rd Co.
Harris, Gideon. Capt. 3rd Co.
Harris, Stephen. 3rd Co.
Hawkins, Jotham. Kimball's Co. 2nd R.I. Regt.
Hawkins, Stephen. 3rd Co.
Henry, Samuel. 5th Co.
Herrenden, John. Capt. 6th Co.
Herrington, Jonathan. Hughes' Co. 2nd R.I. Regt.
Hill, Benjamin.
Hill, John. 1st and 5th Co.
Hill, Rhode.
Hinds, Payne. Humphrey's Co. 2nd R.I. Regt.
Hinds, Richard. Humphrey's Co. 2nd R.I. Regt.
Hines, Pain. Kimball's Co. 2nd R.I. Regt.

Hines, Reuben. Kimball's Co. 2nd R.I. Regt.
Hopkins Jr. Ezekiel. 6th Co.
Hopkins Jr., Timothy. Scituate Hunters. Sgt. Kimball's Co. 2nd
    R.I. Regt. Adjutant. 3rd Providence County Regt.
Hopkins Sr., Ezekiel. 6th Co.
Hopkins, Charles. 6th Co.
Hopkins, Enoch. 6th Co.
Hopkins, Ephrean. Kimball's Co. 2nd R.I. Regt.
Hopkins, Hanan.
Hopkins, Isaac. Lt. Alarm List.
Hopkins, Jebediah. Scituate Hunters.
Hopkins, Jeremiah. 6th Co.
Hopkins, Joel. Kimball's Co. 2nd R.I. Regt.
Hopkins, Jonah. 6th Co.
Hopkins, Maturian. R.I. Regt. of 1781.
Hopkins, Oliver. Kimball's Co. 2nd R.I. Regt.
Hopkins, Pardon. 6th Co.
Hopkins, Peleg. Scituate Hunters.
Hopkins, Reuben. 6th Co.
Hopkins, Richard. C. Olney's Co. 2nd R.I. Regt.
Hopkins, Samuel. 1st Co.
Hopkins, Thomas. Scituate Hunters.
Hopkins, Zebedee. 6th Co.
Horton, Abel. Kimball's Co. 2nd R.I. Regt.
Horton, Benjamin.
Horton, Isaac. 1st Co.
Horton, Jersey.
Horton, Joseph.
Horton, Thomas. Hughes' Co. 2nd R.I. Regt.
Howard, Daniel. Sgt. 2nd Co. Lt. 6th Co.
Howard, James. 2nd Co.
Howard, Silas. Corp. J. Olney's Co. 2nd R.I. Regt.
Howard, William. Capt. 6th Co.
Howland, Edward, 3rd Co.
Hull, Peleg.
Jeffers, Simon. J. Olney's Co. 2nd R.I. Regt.
Jeffers, William. J. Olney's Co. 2nd R.I. Regt.
Jencks, Amos. Lt. J. Olney's Co. 2nd R.I. Regt.

Jencks, Oliver. J. Olney's Co. 2nd R.I. Regt. 1Lt. Shaw's Co. 2nd R.I. Regt. Lt. R.I. Regt. of 1781. Died of disease February 15, 1782 at Philadelphia, Pennsylvania.

Jencks, Samuel.

Johnson, Job. 2nd Co.

Johnson, John. Ens. 2nd Co.

Jones, Abram. Kimball's Co. 2nd R.I. Regt. Thayer's Co. Quebec Expedition.

Kent, Samuel. 5th Co.

Kilton, John I. 1st Co. Captured in 1777, died a prisoner of war at Newport, 1778.

Kimball, Benjamin. 3rd Co.

Kimball, David. Scituate Hunters.

Kimball, Joseph. Capt. Scituate Hunters.

Kimball, Isaac. Scituate Hunters. 3rd Co.

Kimball, Noah. Scituate Hunters. 3rd Co.

Kimball, Samuel. 3rd Co.

Kimball, Stephen. Capt. 2nd R.I. Regt. Capt. Alarm List. Maj. 3rd Providence County Regt.

King, George. J. Olney's Co. 2nd R.I. Regt.

King, Isaac.

King, Peter.

King, Ralph.

King, Samuel. 5th Co.

King, William. J. Olney's Co. 2nd R.I. Regt.

Kinson, William. Surgeon. 3rd Providence County Regt.

Knight Jr., Jonathan. Capt. 1st Co.

Knight Jr., Thomas. Sgt. J. Olney's Co. 2nd R.I. Regt.

Knight, Benajah. 5th Co.

Knight, Christopher. 1st Co.

Knight, David. J. Olney's Co. 2nd R.I. Regt. C. Olney's Co. 2nd R.I. Regt.

Knight, Edward. Capt. 7th Co.

Knight, Edwin. Capt. Alarm List.

Knight, Israel. 5th Co.

Knight, Joseph. Capt. 1st Co. Lt. Col. 3rd Providence County Regt.

Knight, Richard. Sgt. 5th Co. Sgt. Maj. 3rd Providence County Regt.

Knight, Robert. Clerk. 1st Co.
Knight, Rufus. J. Olney's Co. 2nd R.I. Regt.
Knight, Thomas. 1st Co. Sgt. 5th Co.
Knight, William. 1st Co.
Leach, Oliver. 1st Co. Corp. 5th Co. Ens. 1st Co.
Leach, Stephen. 1st and 5th Co.
Lippitt, Moses. Ens. 7th Co.
Lovell, Alexander. 1st and 5th Co.
Lovell, Nathaniel. Lt. Alarm List.
Manchester, Bays.
Manchester, John. 1st Co. J. Olney's Co. 2nd R.I. Regt.
    Potter's Co. 2nd R.I. Regt.
Matthewson, Asa. 5th Co.
Matthewson, Nathan. 1st Co.
Matthewson, Thomas.
Medbury Jr., Isaac. Capt. Scituate Artillery Company.
Medbury, Hezekiah. Kimball's Co. 2nd R.I. Regt.
Medbury, Isaac. Sgt. Kimball's Co. 2nd R.I. Regt.
Medbury, Jonathan. Capt. 7th Co.
Miller, Samuel. R.I. Regt. of 1781.
Miller, William. Sgt. Potter's Co. 2nd R.I. Regt.
Morris, Phillip. J. Olney's Co. 2nd R.I. Regt.
Morris, Samuel. Lt. Scituate Hunters.
Nichols, Caleb. J. Olney's Co. 2nd R.I. Regt.
Olney, Nathan. Sgt. Kimball's Co. 2nd R.I. Regt.
Olney, Richard.
Ormsbury, Elisha. Kimball's Co. 2nd R.I. Regt.
Page, Benjamin. 2nd Co.
Paine, Edward. Corp. Hughes' Co. 2nd R.I. Regt.
Paine, Isaac. Capt. 4th Co.
Paine, Zuriel. 4th Co.
Parker Jr., William. Tew's Co. 2nd R.I. Regt.
Parker, Anthony. 5th Co.
Parker, Francis. 1st Co.
Parker, James. 1st Co.
Parker, John. 1st Co.
Parker, Thomas. 1st Co.
Patrick, James. Potter's Co. 2nd R.I. Regt.
Pearce, Thomas. Kimball's Co. 2nd R.I. Regt.

Peck, Jacob. R.I. Regt. of 1781.
Peckham, Seth. Scituate Hunters.
Perkins, Holmes. Scituate Hunters. Kimball's Co. 2nd R.I.
    Regt.
Perkins, Samuel. Ens. 6th Co.
Peterman, John. 5th Co.
Phillips, Abraham. Corp. Scituate Hunters.
Phillips, John. 5th Co.
Phillips, John. Drummer. 1st Co. J. Olney's Co. 2nd R.I. Regt.
    S. Olney's Co. 2nd R.I. Regt. Gen. Sullivan's Staff.
Phillips, Joslin. 1st Co.
Phillips, Nathaniel. 1st Co.
Phillips, Stephen. Drummer. Allen's Co. 2nd R.I. Regt.
Phillips. William Drummer. Hughes' Co. 2nd R.I. Regt. Died
    May 13, 1778 at Valley Forge.
Pierce, Phillip. 1st Co.
Place, Stephen. 4th Co. Commissary. 3rd Providence County
    Regt.
Potter Jr., Thomas. 5th Co.
Potter, Asa. S. Olney's Co. 2nd R.I. Regt. Killed in Action
    October 22, 1777. Red Bank, New Jersey.
Potter, Caleb. Ens. 3rd Co.
Potter, David. Scituate Hunters.
Potter, Ezra. 6th Co.
Potter, Holiman. Sgt. J. Olney's Co. 2nd R.I. Regt.
Potter, John. Capt. 1st Co.
Potter, John. Captain-Generals Cavaliers.
Potter, Joseph. Ens. 5th Co.
Potter, Moses.
Potter, Nehemiah.
Potter, Phillip. 6th Co.
Potter, Samuel. 5th Co.
Potter, Sylvester. 5th Co.
Potter, William. 4th Co.
Potter, William. Capt. 2nd R.I. Regt.
Potter, Winsor. Scituate Hunters.
Pratt, John. Capt. 3rd Co.
Ralfe, Nathan. Ens. 1st Co. Lt. 5th Co. Capt. 8th Co.
Ralfe, Obadiah. 1st Co.

Ralph Jr., Hugh. 5th Co.
Randall Jr. Job. Scituate Hunters.
Randall, Abner.
Randall, Edward. 5th Co.
Randall, Eleazer. J. Olney's Co. 2nd R.I. Regt.
Randall, Henry. 6th Co.
Randall, Henry. R.I. Regt. of 1781.
Randall, Job. 5th Co.
Randall, John. Potter's Co. 2nd R.I. Regt. R.I. Regt. of 1781.
Randall, Reuben. 5th Co.
Randall, Waterman. J. Olney's Co. 2nd R.I. Regt.
Read, Reuben. Ens. 2nd Co
Remington, Jonathan. 5th Co.
Remington, Joseph. 1st Co.
Remock, David. Kimball's Co. 2nd R.I. Regt.
Rhodes, James. Capt. Alarm List.
Rhodes, Richard. Capt. Alarm List.
Richmond, Ichabod. J. Olney's Co. 2nd R.I. Regt.
Robbins, John. R.I. Regt. of 1781.
Roberts, Collins. 1st Co. J. Olney's Co. 2nd R.I. Regt.
Roberts, Samuel. 5th Co.
Roberts, Thomas. 5th Co.
Rounds, Bertram. Lt. Scituate Hunters.
Rounds, George. Scituate Hunters.
Rounds, John. 4th Co.
Rounds, Levi. 4th Co.
Salisbury Jr. Nathan. 5th Co.
Salisbury, Abel.
Salisbury, Jonathan. Scituate Hunters.
Salisbury, Joseph.
Salisbury, Phillip. 3rd Co. Corp. Kimball's Co. 2nd R.I. Regt
Sarle Jr., Thomas. J. Olney's Co. 2nd R.I. Regt.
Sarle, Elisha. J. Olney's Co. 2nd R.I. Regt.
Saunders, Caleb. 3rd Co.
Saunders, John. Corp. R.I. Regt. of 1781.
Seamens Jr., John. Scituate Hunters.
Seamens, Daniel. Sgt. Scituate Hunters.
Seamens, Thomas. Staff of Maj. Gen. Nathanael Greene.
Seamens, William. 6th Co.

Shalden, Stephen. Capt. 6th Co.

Sheldon, Abel.

Shippey, Israel. Kimball's Co. 2nd R.I. Regt.

Simmons, Benjamin. Clerk. 3rd Co.

Singleton, Samuel. Kimball's Co. 2nd R.I. Regt. Sgt. Thayer's Co. Quebec Expedition. Died in Maine, 1775.

Slack, Benjamin. 6th Co.

Slack, Lemuel. Scituate Hunters.

Smith, Coman. Capt. 3rd Co.

Smith, Hope. Corp. Scituate Hunters.

Smith, John. 3rd Co.

Smith, Jonathan. Lt. Scituate Hunters. Lt. Kimball's Co. 2nd R.I. Regt.

Smith, Oziel. Ens. 6th Co. Lt. 4th Co.

Smith, Patrick.

Smith, Perrigreen. Kimball's Co. 2nd R.I. Regt.

Smith, Resolve.

Smith, Stephen. 6th Co.

Smith, Thomas. Tew's Co. 2nd R.I. Regt.

Smith, William. 3rd Co.

Snow, Zebedee. Lt. 1st Co.

Stafford, William. 1st Co.

Steere, Caleb. 1st Co. J. Olney's Co. 2nd R.I. Regt.

Stone, James. J. Olney's Co. 2nd R.I. Regt.

Stone, Jeremiah. 1st Co. and 1st RI State Regiment.

Swain, John. Kimball's Co. 2nd R.I. Regt.

Sweet, Angell. Lt. 1st Co.

Sylvester, Amos. 5th Co.

Table, Silas. 5th Co.

Tanner, Furmer. 1st Co.

Tanner, Palmer. 5th Co.

Taylor Jr., William. J. Olney's Co. 2nd R.I. Regt.

Taylor, Benjamin. 6th Co. Scituate Hunters.

Taylor, Elisha. R.I. Regt. of 1781.

Taylor, James. Ens. 2nd Co.

Taylor, Job.

Taylor, John. S. Olney's Co. 2nd R.I. Regt.

Taylor, Nathaniel. Allen's Co. 2nd R.I. Regt.

Taylor, Thomas. R.I. Regt. of 1781.

Taylor, William. 1st Co.

Tewgood, Jonathan. 6th Co.

Thomas, Nicholas. 5th Co.

Thornton, Stuckely. 1st Co. J. Olney's Co. 2nd R.I. Regt.

Thornton, Thomas. Kimball's Co. 2nd R.I. Regt.

Tripp, Benjamin. 2nd Co.

Turner, Joseph. 1st Co. Shaw's Co. 2nd R.I. Regt. Died April
    31, 1778 at Valley Forge.

Tyler, James. Ens. 2nd Co.

Vaughn, William. 5th Co.

Walker, George.

Walker, Jacob. Scituate Hunters.

Walker, John. Kimball's Co. 2nd R.I. Regt.

Walker, Nathan. 1st Co.

Walker, Phillip. Ens. 4th Co.

Walker, William. Ens. 4th Co.

Walling, Jeremiah. Kimball's Co. 2nd R.I. Regt.

Waterman, Nathan. Fifer. J. Olney's Co. 2nd R.I. Regt.

Weatherhead, Comfort. Kimball's Co. 2nd R.I. Regt.

Weaver, Thomas. J. Olney's Co. 2nd R.I. Regt.

Weeks, Oliver. J. Olney's Co. 2nd R.I. Regt.

Wells, James. Ens. Alarm List. Lt. 6th Co.

Wells, John. 1st and 5th Co.

West, John. Scituate Hunters. Potter's Co. 2nd R.I. Regt.

West, Thomas. Scituate Hunters.

West, William. Col. 3rd Providence County Regt. Brig. Gen.
    Providence County Brigade.

Westcott, Caleb. Scituate Hunters. Ens. 3rd Co.

Westcott, Eleazor. 1st Co.

Westcott, James. Kimball's Co. 2nd R.I. Regt.

Westcott, Jeremiah. Kimball's Co. 2nd R.I. Regt.

Westcott, Josiah.

Westcott, Jr. Oliver. Scituate Hunters.

Westcott, Stuckly. J. Olney's Co. 2nd R.I. Regt.

Westcott, Ziba. R.I. Regt. of 1781.

Wheaton, James. 5th Co.

Whipple, Benjamin. 5th Co.

Whipple, Benedict.

Whipple, Joel. J. Olney's Co. 2nd R.I. Regt.

Whipple, John. S. Olney's Co. 2nd R.I. Regt.
Whipple, John. 2nd Co.
White Jr., John. 5th Co.
White, Aaron, 5th Co.
White, Jospeh. 5th Co.
White, Nathan. J. Olney's Co. 2nd R.I. Regt.
Whitman, Benajah. 5th Co.
Whitman, David. Kimball's Co. 2nd R.I. Regt. Hughes' Co.
    2nd R.I. Regt. Died 1778 at Valley Forge.
Whitman, John. Kimball's Co. 2nd R.I. Regt.
Whitman, Stephen. Scituate Hunters.
Whitmore, Benjamin. 1st Co.
Whitmore, David. Hughes' Co. 2nd R.I. Regt.
Wight, David. Ens. 1st Co.
Wight, Joseph. 1st Co.
Wight, Samuel. 1st Co.
Wilbur, Abner. 5th Co.
Wilbur, Knight. 1st Co.
Wilbur, John. 5th Co.
Wilbur, Samuel. Capt. 1st and 5th Co.
Wilbur, Semour. 5th Co.
Wilbur, Simeon. Sgt. 1st Co.
Wilkinson, John. Surgeon's Mate. 3rd Providence County
    Regt.
Williams, Benjamin. 3rd Co.
Williams, James. Capt. 3rd Co.
Williams, Joseph. Kimball's Co. 2nd R.I. Regt.
Williams, Squire. Alarm List. Maintained Scituate Beacon.
Wood, Amos. 5th Co.
Wood, Benjamin. 1st Co. Corp. J. Olney's Co. 2nd R.I. Regt.
    Sgt. 5th Co.
Wood, Ezekiel. 1st Co.
Wood, James. 5th Co. J. Olney's Co. 2nd R.I. Regt. S. Olney's
    Co. 2nd R.I. Regt.
Wood, John. 5th Co. S. Olney's Co. 2nd R.I. Regt.
Wood, Jonathan. 1st Co. Army of Observation.
Wood, Stephen. 4th Co.
Wood, William. 2nd Co.
Worker, Nathan. Capt. Alarm List.

Wright, Zephaniah. 4th Co.
Yain, John. 5th Co.
Yaw, David. 1st Co.
Young, Joel. 5th Co.
Young, Joseph. 5th Co.
Young, Stephen. Sgt. 5th Co.

NOTES

CHAPTER ONE

[1] C.C. Beaman, *An Historical Address, delivered in Scituate, Rhode Island, July 4, 1876* (Phenix, R.I.: Capron & Campbell Steam Book and Job Printers, 1877), 10-11.

[2] Charles K, Bennet and J. Michael Lenihan, *A History of Scituate, R.I., Being an account of its Early Settlement and Events to the Present* (North Scituate, R.I.: Copy World, 1977), 32. Little is known about the tribe, and no archaeological evidence has ever been uncovered, save for occasional arrowheads and pottery shards unearthed while farming. In all probability they were members of the Nipmuc, who were known inhabitants of the area.

[3] Beaman, 8-11.

[4] *Records of the Colony of Rhode Island and Providence Plantations in New England,* John Russell Bartlett, ed. (Providence: A. Crawford and Greene, 1862), vol. 7, 299. All references are for this volume.; *The Rhode Island 1777 Military Census*, Mildred M. Chamberlain, ed. (Baltimore: Genealogical Publishing Co., 1985) 269.

[5] Knight Oral History as told by Joyce Knight Townsend.

[6] Beaman, 32-36. As the tavern would burn down before the advent of photography, this description has been given to give the reader a sense of how the Angell Tavern appeared.

CHAPTER TWO

[1] Joseph Jencks Smith, *Civil and Military List of Rhode Island, 1647-1800* (Providence: Preston and Rounds, 1900), 215; Hedley Smith, *The History of Scituate, Rhode Island* (C.T.: Racine Publishing, 1976), 32. Many of these men received grants for one hundred acres around Darby, Vermont, where their descendents still live.

[2] Beaman, 41; Knight Oral History as told by Joyce Knight Townsend.

[3] Hedley Smith, 73; "An Act Incorporating a Military Company named the Scituate Hunters." Rhode Island State Archives. Providence, Rhode Island.

[4] "Scituate Hunters."

[5] Joseph Jencks Smith, 305.

[6] Joseph Jencks Smith, 306.

[7] Bartlett, 358-359.

CHAPTER THREE

[1] Bartlett, 264.

[2] Edward Field, *Revolutionary Defenses in Rhode Island* (Providence: Preston and Rounds, 1896), 1-4; " Scituate Hunters"; Erich O. A. D'Taylor, *Campaign on Rhode Island: 1778* (Newport, R.I.: NP, 1978), 9. Some companies often had as many as twenty officers, and no privates. In 1778 the Rhode Island General Assembly stepped in, and only allowed one commissioned officer to every thirty privates.

[3] Bartlett, 264; *The Manual Exercise as ordered by His Majesty in 1764 and including the Fundamentals of marching and military marching and maneuvering,* Mark R. Tully, ed. (Baraboo, W.I.: Ballindalloch Press, 2001), 1.

[4] Field, *Defenses*, 37.

[5] Frank J. Kravic and George C. Neumann, *Collector's Illustrated Encyclopedia of the American Revolution* (Texarkana, T.X.: Scurlock Publishing, 1997); Field, *Defenses,* 14-41.

[6] Field, *Defenses*, 3. The type of musket the militia carried was not specified by the state. Some companies had over a dozen different types of muskets, each using a different type of ammunition. Many men were simply given a bar of lead, and told to cast their own bullets. The Rhode Island militia seldom carried bayonets.

[7] Earl J. Coates and James L. Kochan, *Don Troiani's Soldiers in America: 1753-1865* (Mechanicsburg, P.A.: Stackpole Books, 1998), 53.

[8] Kravic and Neumann, 125-127.

[9] Bartlett, 264. These weapons, along with other town stock were held at the Angell Tavern.

[10] Kravic and Neumann, 148-155; "Will of Joseph Knight", author's collection. In the 1920s, after the building of the Scituate Reservoir, many Knights left Scituate for western Massachusetts, taking with them Captain Knight's sword, musket, and powder horn, along with most of his papers.

[11] Field, *Defenses,* 14-42.

CHAPTER FOUR

[1] Bartlett, 283.

[2] Hedley Smith, 72.

[3] Margery I. Matthews, *Foster and the Patriot's Dream: A Bicentennial Reflection* (Foster, R.I.: Foster Preservation Society, 1976), 9. It is unclear as to Boswell's reason for choosing Scituate, but there was a large network in place to help British soldiers escape from Boston. It is also unclear what regiment Boswell came from, or when he came to North America. Based on his account of when he came to America it is believed he served in the 10th or 52nd Regiment.

[4] Beaman, 43-44.

[5] Joseph Knight to Robert Knight (April 11, 1775), author's collection. It is unknown if Phillips or Yaw paid the fines, as they were dropped from the rolls in early April. Perhaps they might have been Tories. Manchester paid the fine, and signed the roll on April 20, 1775.

[6] Field, *Defenses,* 1-4. Powder was at a premium, and the fines collected bought much needed powder and lead for the militia to train with.

[7] Beaman, 43. There is no doubting the claim that Fisk was very wealthy. He owned over 1,000 acres in Scituate and Cranston. A pair of his breeches buckles in the possession of the Nathanael Greene Homestead are made out of solid silver, with gold tongues, quite a lavish expenditure for the time.

[8] Hedley Smith, 73.

CHAPTER FIVE

[1] David Hackett Fischer, *Paul Revere's Ride* (New York: Oxford University Press, 1994).

[2] Ruth Boss, "Scituate in the Revolutionary War" North Scituate Public Library. North Scituate, Rhode Island.

[3] Beaman, 41-43; Field, *Defenses,* 5-13; Benjamin Colwell, *Spirit of '76 in Rhode Island* (Boston: A.J. Wright, Printer, 1850.), 13. Only Captain Knight and Surgeon Fisk signed their ranks to the roll. The author added the others in parentheses. Out of seventy-six men in the company, only fifty-two responded to the call. It is interesting to note that both Boss and Knight were planting when the rider appeared. That is a clear indication of an early planting that year, as most Scituate farmers had not put in their seeds until the end of April.

[4] Bartlett, 316-346.

[5] Field, *Defenses,* 5-13; Anthony Walker, *So Few the Brave* (Newport: R.I.: Seafield Press, 1981), 8.

[6] Field, *Defenses,* 13. In tribute to these two men of Scituate, who are still declared missing in action, the author erected a memorial stone in their memory in the North Scituate Cemetery.

[7] Field, *Defenses,* 55; Matthews, 8.

CHAPTER SIX

[1] Joseph Jencks Smith, 321.
[2] Beaman, 41-42. This letter offers some good evidence that the Second Company of Minutemen could be depended upon.
[3] Charles G. Maytum, *Early Prudence Island* (Portsmouth R.I.: NP, 1963), 77.
[4] Maytum, 79-82.
[5] Beaman, 42.
[6] Maytum, 82-86. It is interesting to note how Wallace describes how the Militia fought, as well as overestimating their numbers. On the first day, no more than 75 men were engaged, and on the second day, no more than 150. Perhaps because they fought so well, Wallace overestimated the numbers. Today the battlefield is a Rhode Island State Park, and a small marker placed by the Daughters of the American Revolution indicates the location.
[7] Joseph Jencks Smith, 331.
[8] Beaman, 43.
[9] Philip Brown, Pension File. National Archives. Washington D.C.
[10] Anthony Walker, 18-19.
[11] Anthony Walker, 15-27; Boss, "Revolutionary War". Boss wrote home constantly about his experiences during the war. Afterwards he wrote a manuscript about his experiences. Unfortunately, as with most of the accounts written by Revolutionary Veterans it has been lost to the ravages of time.

CHAPTER SEVEN

[1] Don N. Hagist, *General Orders, Rhode Island December 1776-January 1778* (Bowie, M.D.: Heritage Books, Inc, 2001), 1.
[2] Brown, Pension File. Brown's Pension File provides perhaps the best information on the inside workings of the Rhode Island Militia during the Revolution.
[3] "Payment returns", author's collection.
[4] "Minutes of Town Council Meeting, April 28, 1777." author's collection. Hadley Smith, 78-84.
[5] "Deposition pertaining to Oliver Fisk.", author's collection. Fisk's remains have never been located. They probably lie in a tomb in New

York, where the remains of over three thousand American prisoners of war reside.

[6] Joseph Jencks Smith, 367. Colonel Colwell was placed in command of the defenses of Providence, located at Field's Point.

[7] "Return for the Campaign upon Rhode Island.", author's collection.

[8] Bartlett, 358-359. With these changes the companies simply reverted to their original designation before the minutemen were activated.

CHAPTER EIGHT

[1] Hedley Smith, 77.

[2] Beaman, 42.

[3] George M. West, *William West of Scituate, Rhode Island: Farmer, Soldier, Statesmen* (St. Andrews, F.L.: Panama City Publishing Co., 1919), 18.

[4] Beaman, 42. Flax was very scarce, as it was the raw form of linen, from which many articles of clothing were made. As such, it was severely rationed for the Continentals, and Rhode Island Militia officers, making it available to Major Knight.

[5] West, 8.

[6] Beaman, 32-36.

CHAPTER NINE

[1] Hedley Smith, 63; Beaman, 62-65.

[2] Field, *Defenses*, 53. The cannon were set up at the various choke points along Narragansett Bay. Some cannon were later cast and put onto Newport, and were captured when Newport fell in 1776.

[3] Scituate Preservation Society, *Discover Hope Village* (Providence: Rhode Island Historical Preservation and Heritage Commission, 1996), 6-7. To this day, people in Hope continue to find cannon balls in their yards, while the bluff the cannon were proofed upon is now a park. The cannon in front of the Hope Library is believed to be one of the field guns attached to the regiment.

[4] Scituate Preservation Society, 8-9.

CHAPTER TEN

[1] Anthony Walker, 35.

[2] Anthony Walker, 34; Boss, *Revolutionary War*; Scituate Militia papers in the possession of the author.

[3] Anthony Walker, 39.

[4] Anthony Walker, 40-42.

[5] Anthony Walker, 40-42; Boss, Revolutionary War. Catherine R. Williams. Biography of Revolutionary Heroes; Containing the Life of Brigadier Gen. William Barton, and Also, of Captain Stephen Olney. [New York: Wiley & Putnam, 1839], 226-227.

[6] Boss, "Revolutionary War".

[7] Anthony Walker, 45. The clothing issued consisted of a white linen frock coat, white linen overalls or gaitered trousers, and black cocked hats.

[8] Boss, "Revolutionary War".

[9] Jeremiah Greenman, *Diary of a Common Soldier in the American Revolution, 1775-1783: An Annotated Edition of the Military Journal of Jeremiah Greenman,* edited by Robert Bray and Paul Bushnell (De Kalb, I.L.: Northern Illinois University Press, 1978), 125. These two regiments had previously been in Boston, guarding the prisoners captured at Saratoga. Sherburne's was assigned to Varnum's Brigade, while Webb's was assigned to Glover's Brigade. The men of the Second Rhode Island washed their clothes in the Ponagansett River. The place where they encamped can still be seen today, although it is now underwater, along with the Angell Tavern.

[10] Anthony Walker, 63.

[11] "Return of men for the Second Regiment.", author's collection.

[12] Anthony Walker, 71-73.

[13] Anthony Walker, 72-73.

[14] Hedley Smith, 87; Anthony Walker, 81.

[15] Anthony Walker, 87.

CHAPTER ELEVEN

[1] Beaman, 42; Matthews, 9; "Ration returns." author's collection.

[2] Beaman, 43; Joseph Jencks Smith, 367; Taylor, 15.

[3] Anthony Walker, 52-56.

[4] Anthony Walker, 54-58; John Sullivan, *Letters and papers of Major General John Sullivan, Continental Army: Volume Two, 1778-1779,* edited by Otis G. Hammond (Concord, N.H.: New Hampshire Historical Society, 1931), 254-255.

[5] West, 19; Anthony Walker, 57.

[6] Anthony Walker, 62-64.

[7] West, 19; Brown, Pension File; Frederic Mackenzie, *The Diary of Frederic Mackenzie,* edited by Allen French. (Cambridge, M.A.: Harvard University Press, 1930), Vol. 2.; Matthews, 9. It is a very interesting that with close to 8,000 men present with the Continentals, the State Brigade, and other Rhode Island Militia units, Lafayette would select West's Brigade for the most hazardous position on the line. Perhaps he had heard of their previous reputation. In any case, West's Brigade held their position all night, in a very dangerous position. It is unclear as the amount of casualties suffered, or to which regiments they belonged.

[8] West, 19; Beaman, 44-45; Joseph Jencks Smith, 367.

CHAPTER TWELVE

[1] Edwin Martin Stone, *Our French Allies* (Providence: Providence Press Company, 1884), 133-160.

[2] Beaman, 43.

[3] Stone.

[4] Matthews, 8-9. In all truth these stories are probably correct.

[5] Hedley Smith, 78-79. The French soldier was removed to the Rockland Cemetery in 1921. His remains have never been identified. It is claimed the Marquis de Lafayette left a large sum of money with a local townsmen to purchase an appropriate grave marker for his soldier, but no marker was ever purchased. In 1824 Lafayette returned to America, and during a tour of Rhode Island, stopped at the Angell Tavern.

[6] Stone, 392-430.

CHAPTER THIRTEEN

[1] Bennet and Lenihan, 42.

[2] Joseph Jencks Smith, 454.

[3] Bennet and Lenihan, 76-78.

[4] Knight Oral History as told by Joyce Knight Townsend. The Knight cemeteries are owned by the Providence Water Supply Board. They are in a poor shape of disrepair. The Water Supply Board "is not responsible for their maintenance."

EPILOUGUE

[1] Scituate, Rhode Island. Town Records. Town Clerk's Office. North Scituate, Rhode Island.

[2] Ibid. Hedley Smith. 86-87.

[3] Foster, Rhode Island. Town Records. Town Clerk's Office. Foster, Rhode Island.

[4] Ibid.

[5] Bennet and Lenihan. 55-56.

[6] Scituate, Rhode Island. Town Records. Town Clerk's Office. North Scituate, Rhode Island.

[7] Ibid.

[8] Ibid.

[9] Ibid. Scituate Militia papers in the in the possession of the author.

[10] Ibid.

[11] Ibid.

[12] Foster, Rhode Island. Town Records. Town Clerk's Office. Foster, Rhode Island.

[13] Scituate, Rhode Island. Town Records. Town Clerk's Office. North Scituate, Rhode Island.

[14] Ibid.

BIBLIOGRAPHY

Manuscripts and Unpublished Works

Boss, Ruth C. *Scituate in the Revolutionary War.* 1930. North Scituate Public Library. North Scituate, Rhode Island.

Brown, Phillip. Pension File. National Archives.

Foster, Rhode Island. Town Records. Town Clerk's Office. Foster, Rhode Island.

Knight Papers. Author's Collection. Warwick, Rhode Island.

Najecki, Roy P. *Light Infantry Tactics.* 2000. Private Collection. Chepachet, Rhode Island.

Najecki, Roy P. *A Short History of the 2nd Rhode Island Regiment of the Continental Line.* 1983. Private Collection. Chepachet, Rhode Island.

Rhode Island Militia Papers. Rhode Island State Archives. Providence, Rhode Island.

Scituate, Rhode Island. Militia Papers. Author's Collection. Warwick, Rhode Island.

Scituate, Rhode Island. Town Records. Town Clerk's Office. North Scituate, Rhode Island.

Sullivan Papers. Rhode Island State Archives. Providence, Rhode Island.

Townsend, Joyce Knight. Interviews pertaining to the Knight family. 2000-2005.

Walker, Cyrus. *History of Scituate, Rhode Island.* 1890. Town Clerk's Office. North Scituate, Rhode Island.

Primary Sources

Andre, John. *Journal.* Edited by William Abbatt. New York: Arno Press, 1968.

Angell, Israel. *Diary of Colonel Israel Angell.* Edited by Edward Field. Providence: Preston and Rounds, 1899.

Beaman, C.C. *An Historical Address Delivered in Scituate, Rhode Island, July 4th, 1776*. Phenix, R.I.: Capron and Campbell Steam Book and Job Printers, 1877.

Burgess, Gideon A. *The Owen Soldiers Monument, North Scituate Rhode Island*. North Scituate, R.I.: E.F. Sibley and Co., 1913.

David, Ebenezer. *A Rhode Island Chaplain in the Revolution: Letters of Ebenezer David to Nicolas Brown, 1775-1778*. Edited by Jeanette D. Black and William G. Roelker. London: Kennikat Press, 1972.

Greenman, Jeremiah. *Diary of Common Soldier in the American Revolution: An Annotated Edition of the Military Journal of Jeremiah Greenman*. Edited by Robert Bray and Paul Bushnell. DeKalb, I.L.: Northern Illinois University Press, 1978.

Mackenzie, Frederic. *The Diary of Frederic Mackenzie*. Edited by Allen French. Cambridge, M.A.: Harvard University Press, 1930.

Martin, Joseph Plumb. *Narrative of a Revolutionary Soldier*. New York: Signet Classic, 2001.

Pickering, Timothy. *An Easy plan for the Discipline of a Militia*. Salem, M.A.: NP, 1775.

Potter, Jeremiah. *Genealogy of the Potter Family*. Phenix, R.I.: John H. Campbell Book and Job Printer, 1881)

State of Rhode Island. *Records of the Colony of Rhode Island and Providence Plantations in New England*. Edited by John Russell Bartlett. Providence: A. Crawford Greene, 1862.

State of Rhode Island. *The Rhode Island 1777 Military Census.* Transcribed by Mildred M. Chamberlain. Baltimore: Genealogical Publishing, 1985.

Sullivan, John. *Letters and Papers of Major General John Sullivan, Continental Army: Volume Two, 1778-1779*. Edited by Otis G. Hammond. Concord, N.H.: New Hampshire Historical Society, 1931.

Taylor, Maureen Alice. *Runaways, Deserters, and Notorious Villains*. Rockport, M.E.: Picton Press, 1994.

The Manual Exercise as Ordered by His Majesty in 1764 and including the Fundamentals of Marching and Maneuverings. Edited by Mark R. Tully. Baraboo, W.I.: Ballindalloch Press, 2001.

Williams, Catherine R. *Biography of Revolutionary Heroes; Containing the Life of Brigadier Gen. William Barton, and Also, of Captain Stephen Olney.* New York: Wiley & Putnam, 1839.

Secondary Sources

Achtermier, William O. *Rhode Island Arms Makers and Gunsmiths: 1643-1883.* Providence: Mobary, 1980.

Bennet, Charles K. and J. Michael Lenihan. *A History of Scituate Rhode Island: Being an Account of its Early Settlement and Events to the Present.* North Scituate, R.I.: Copy World, 1977.

Birnbaum, Louis. *Red Dawn at Lexington.* Boston: Houghton Mifflin, 1986.

Bolton, Charles K. *The Private Soldier under Washington.* Gansevoort, N.Y.: Corner House Historical Publications, 1997.

Coates, Earl J. and James L. Kochan. *Don Troiani's Soldiers in America: 1753-1865.* Mechanicsburg, P.A.: Stackpole Books, 1998.

Coburn, Frank W. *The Battle of April 19, 1775.* London: Kennikat Press, 1970.

Colwell, Benjamin. *Spirit of '76 in Rhode Island.* Boston: A.J. Wright, Printer, 1850.

Curtis, Edward E. *The British Army in the American Revolution.* Gansevoort, N.Y.: Corner House Historical Publications, 1998.

Darling, Anthony D. *Redcoat and Brown Bess.* Canada: Museum Restoration Service, 1971.

Dearden, Paul F. *The Rhode Island Campaign of 1778: Inauspicious Dawn of Alliance.* Providence: Rhode Island Bicentennial Foundation, 1987.

Field, Edward. *The Colonial Tavern: A Glimpse of New England Town Life in the Seventeenth and Eighteenth Centuries.* Providence: Preston and Rounds, 1897.

Field, Edward. *Esek Hopkins: Commander in Chief of the Continental Navy during the American Revolution: 1775-1778.* Providence: Preston and Rounds, 1898.

Field, Edward. *Revolutionary Defenses in Rhode Island.* Providence: Preston and Rounds, 1896.

Fischer, David Hackett. *Paul Revere's Ride.* New York: Oxford University Press, 1994.

Fischer, David Hackett. *Washington's Crossing.* New York: Oxford University Press, 2004.

Hagist, Don N. *General Orders, Rhode Island: December 1776-January 1778.* Bowie, M.D.: Heritage Books, 2001.

Heritage Room Committee. *Images of America: Scituate, R.I.* Great Britain: Arcadia Publishing 1998.

Ketchum, Richard M. *Saratoga: Turning Point of America's Revolution.* New York: Henry Holt and Co., 1997.

Lovejoy, David S. *Rhode Island Politics and the American Revolution.* Providence: Brown University Press, 1958.

Lovell, Louise Lewis. *Israel Angell, Colonel of the 2nd Rhode Island Regiment.* New York: Knickerbocker Press, 1921.

Lowell, Edward J. *The Hessians and Other German Auxiliaries of Great Britain in the Revolutionary War.* Gansevoort, N.Y.: Corner House Historical Publications, 1997.

May, Robin. *The British Army in North America: 1775-83.* Oxford: Osprey Publishing, 1999.

Maytum, Charles G. *Early Prudence Island.* Portsmouth, R.I.: NP, 1963.

Matthews, Margery I. *Foster and the Patriot's Dream: A Bicentennial Reflection.* Foster, R.I.: Foster Preservation Society, 1976.

Neumann, George C. and Frank J. Kravic. *Collector's Illustrated Encyclopedia of the American Revolution.* Texarkana, T.X.: Scurlock Publishing, 1997.

Reed, Joseph. *Valley Forge: Crucible of Victory.* Monmouth, N.J.: Phillip Freneau Press, 1969.

Reid, Stuart. *British Redcoat.* Oxford: Osprey Publishing, 1996.

Schultz, Eric B. and Michael J. Tougias. *King Phillip's War: The History and Legacy of America's Forgotten Conflict.* Woodstock, V.T.: The Countryman Press, 1999.

Scituate Preservation Society. *Discover Hope Village.* Providence: Rhode Island Historical Preservation and Heritage Commission, 1996.

Simister, Florence P. *The Fire's Center: Rhode Island in the Revolutionary Era, 1763-1790.* Providence: Rhode Island Bicentennial Foundation, 1979.

Smith, Hedley. *The History of Scituate, Rhode Island.* C.T.: Racine Printing, 1976.

Smith, Joseph Jencks. *Civil and Military List of Rhode Island: 1647-1800.* Providence: Preston and Rounds, 1900.

Smith, Samuel Stelle. *The Battle of Monmouth.* Monmouth, N.J.: Phillip Freneau Press, 1964.

Smith, Samuel Stelle. *The Battle of Princeton.* Monmouth, N.J.: Phillip Freneau Press, 1967.

Smith, Samuel Stelle. *The Battle of Trenton.* Monmouth, N.J.: Phillip Freneau Press, 1965.

Smith, Samuel Stelle. *Fight for the Delaware 1777.* Monmouth, N.J.: Phillip Freneau Press, 1970.

Stone, Edwin M. *Our French Allies.* Providence: Providence Press, 1884.

Taaffe, Stephen R. *The Philadelphia Campaign: 1777-1778.* Lawrence, K.S.: University Press of Kansas, 2003.

Taylor, Erich A.O.D. *Campaign on Rhode Island: 1778.* Newport: NP, 1978.

United States Department of the Interior. *Morristown: Official National Park Handbook.* Washington D.C.: Division of Publications: National Park Service, 1983.

Walker, Anthony. *So Few the Brave.* Newport: Seafield Press, 1981.

Walker, Edwin Robert, et al., eds. *A History of Trenton: 1679-1929, Two hundred and fifty years of a Notable Town with Links in Four Centuries.* Princeton, N.J.: Princeton University Press, 1929.

West, George M. *William West of Scituate, R.I.: Farmer, Soldier, Statesman.* St. Andrews, F.L.: Panama City Publishing, 1919.

ABOUT THE AUTHOR

Robert Grandchamp is a twelfth-generation Rhode Islander, and a descendent of Colonel Joseph Knight. He is presently enrolled at Rhode Island College, majoring in Secondary Education and Antropology. Mr. Grandchamp enjoys Revolutionary and Civil War living history, as well as traveling to battlefields of all wars. He resides in Warwick, Rhode Island.

I N D E X

This index does not include the alphabetical list of names in the appendix.

Varnum's Rhode Island Brigade 49 at Peekskill NY and Camden NJ 46
Vermont Land Grants (for Militia Service), 5
Vernon, xii
Von Donop, Col Carl; Attempted to Storm Fort Mercer 46
Von Steuben, Baron; at Valley Forge 47
Walker, Nathan 19
Wallace, Capt James 24 25 27
Wanton, Gov Joseph Exiled 24
War of 1812, Scituate Service 67
Warren RI, Cannon Defense 41
Warwick Neck, 24 Cannon Defense 41
Washington, General George xi 23 52 55 57 at Trenton 28 at Yorktown 43 Crossing Delaware River 59 Defeated at Brandywine and Germantown 46 Speaks to Benjamin Boss at Valley

Forge 47 Traveled Through Scituate 28
West, Brig Gen William 24 31 34 37 39 57 72 Col Wm 7 20 Promoted to Brig Gen 23 Home of (Photograph) 38
Westcott, Eleazor 20
Whitmore, Benjamin 20
Wight, Joseph 24
Wilbur, Capt Samuel 27 31 56 72
Wilbur, Knight 27
Wilbur, Lt Samuel 16 19
Wilbur, Sgt Simeon 20 24
Wilbur Hollow RI, xii 2 Flooded for Reservoir 68
Williams, Squire 21
Women, Support Roles Performed During Revolution 37
Wood, Cpl Benjamin 19 21
Wood, Ezekiel 20
Yaw, David; Fined for Failure to Appear 16 17
Yorktown Rhode Island Regiment at, 52

www.ingramcontent.com/pod-product-compliance
Lightning Source LLC
Chambersburg PA
CBHW060405090426
42734CB00011B/2268